Pelican Books
Practical Thinking:
Four ways to be right;
Five ways to be wrong;
Five ways to understand

Edward de Bono was born in Malta and after his initial education at St Edward's College, Malta, and the Royal University of Malta, where he obtained a degree in medicine, he proceeded as a Rhodes Scholar to Christ Church, Oxford, where he gained an honours degree in psychology and physiology and then a D.Phil. in medicine. He also holds a Ph.D. from Cambridge. He has had faculty appointments at the universities of Oxford, London, Cambridge and Harvard.

Dr de Bono is the founder and director of the Cognitive Research Trust in Cambridge (founded 1969) and the Centre for the Study of Thinking. He runs what is now the largest curriculum programme in the world for the direct teaching of thinking in schools. Dr de Bono's instruction in thinking has been sought by many of the leading corporations such as IBM, Shell, Unilever, ICI, Du Pont and many others. He has been invited to lecture extensively throughout the world.

He has written many books which have been translated into nineteen languages. He has also completed two TV series 'The Greatest Thinkers' for WDR, Germany, and 'De Bono's Course in Thinking' for the BBC. Dr de Bono is the originator of the term 'lateral thinking' and also the inventor of the classic L-game which is said to be the simplest real game ever invented.

His books include *The Use of Lateral Thinking* (1967), *The Five-Day Course in Thinking* (1968), *The Mechanism of Mind* (1969), *The Dog-Exercising Machine* (1970), *Technology Today* (1971), *Practical Thinking* (1971), *Lateral Thinking for Management* (1971), *Po: Beyond Yes and No* (1972), *Children Solve Problems* (1972), *Eureka!: An Illustrated History of Inventions from the Wheel to the Computer* (1974). *Teaching Thinking* (1976), *The Greatest Thinkers* (1976), *Wordpower* (1977), *The Happiness Purpose* (1977), *Opportunities: A Handbook of Business Opportunity Search* (1978), *Future Positive* (1979), *Atlas of Management Thinking* (1981), and *De Bono's Course in Thinking* (1982). Many of these have been published in Penguin. Dr de Bono has also contributed to many journals, including the *Lancet* and *Clinical Science*. He is married and has two sons.

Edward de Bono

Practical Thinking

4 ways to be right.   5 ways to be wrong.   5 ways to understand

Penguin Books

Penguin Books Ltd, Harmondsworth, Middlesex, England
Viking Penguin Inc., 40 West 23rd Street, New York, New York 10010, U.S.A.
Penguin Books Australia Ltd, Ringwood, Victoria, Australia
Penguin Books Canada Ltd, 2801 John Street, Markham, Ontario, Canada L3R 1B4
Penguin Books (N.Z.) Ltd, 182–190 Wairau Road, Auckland 10, New Zealand

First published by Jonathan Cape 1971
Published in Pelican Books 1976
Reprinted 1976, 1977, 1978, 1979, 1981, 1983, 1985

Set, printed and bound in Great Britain by
Cox & Wyman Ltd, Reading
Set in Monotype Times

Contents

Introduction

How is it that in a fight both sides are always right? How is it that no one ever makes a mistake on purpose but mistakes get made all the time?

Everyday thinking is what fills in the time when you are neither asleep nor dead. Just as you notice a car engine only when it is not running smoothly so you become aware of everyday thinking when it is not running smoothly. Everyday thinking is involved in family squabbles; making mayonnaise; planning a holiday; what to do about the dog when you want to go away for the week-end; thinking of an excuse for getting to work late; finding an easy way of getting through your work; educating the children; opening a bottle of beer when you have lost the opener; keeping your end up in a political argument; and possibly trying to make the world a better place to live in.

There is no law requiring one to think for oneself or to make one's own ideas. In important matters it is usually easier to accept other people's ideas ready-made and this saves one the trouble of doing any thinking for oneself – though one may still have to do it in minor matters. Often one has no choice but to accept the ideas of others because thinking things out for oneself can be so difficult. Education unfortunately provides little help in this matter. You can probably remember things you were taught at school about geography (valleys, river deltas, rice-growing countries, etc.)

and about history (dates of battles, names of kings, etc.). But can you remember what you were taught about thinking? Or is thinking something that one knows all about anyway – like walking or breathing?

The truth is that thinking is too important a matter to do anything about. So we have left it to the philosophers who over the ages have amused themselves with the most intricate analyses which have little relevance to everyday life. Some time ago a man,* who was described as being one of the most influential philosophers of the century, died. Influential on his fellow philosophers, but hardly on anyone else. Just how much influence does logical positivism have on everyday thinking?

In everyday thinking both sides in a fight are always right. This is because being right is the *feeling* of being right. This is what guides your actions, not the abstract philosophical rightness of your ideas. In this book the four practical ways of being right are explored: currant cake (emotional rightness); jig-saw puzzle (logical rightness); village Venus (unique rightness); measles (recognition rightness). In addition to picking out and naming the four different ways of being right the book also picks out and names the five levels of understanding and the five major mistakes in thinking.

The purpose of picking out and naming these patterns of thinking is to make them recognizable. It then becomes possible to recognize these patterns in your own thinking and in the thinking of others. You can also talk about them in as definite a way as you might talk about a car or a hamburger. Without such named patterns thinking is vague and intangible and hence very difficult to talk about.

As soon as one can talk about thinking one is on the way to regarding it as a skill like playing tennis or cooking. Far too many people regard thinking as a matter of inborn intelligence – which it is not. In my researches and experiments I have again and again come across very intelligent people who

* Rudolf Carnap.

turned out to be very poor thinkers. Nor have I found that thinking skill has much to do with education, for some of the best educated people (Ph.D.s, university lecturers and professors, senior business executives, etc.) have also been poor thinkers. To regard thinking as a skill rather than as a gift is the first step towards doing something to improve that skill.

The book looks at practical everyday thinking which allows us to use something effectively without knowing all the details – for instance a TV set. Other aspects of thinking explored include imagination, creativity, the YES/NO system, the deadly danger of arrogance and the huge importance of humour in thinking.

Thinking may seem to be too complex a process to be understood but the two basic steps are quite simple. The book also explains the extraordinary paradox that man may be able to think so much better than animals only because he is *stupider*.

In writing about thinking it is very easy to get lost in word dances with ideas chasing ideas in a confused whirl. In order to avoid this confusion the book is based on a direct experiment in thinking and not on fancy speculation. This simple experiment provides the backbone that runs through the book and keeps it from flopping into a shapeless metaphysical mess.

I really do believe that the most optimistic thing about the human race is its relative stupidity. There would be little hope if the human race was as bright as it thinks it is and still got itself into so much trouble. I believe that if we started paying attention directly to the subject of everyday thinking it would be rather more useful than shooting for the moon. At the moment, for instance, there are more professors in England concerned with Sanskrit than with thinking as a skill.

Knowing What to Do

Instinct · Learning · Understanding

Thinking is that waste of time between seeing something and knowing what to do about it. The time is filled with ideas which lead on from one to another as we try and sort out the unfamiliar situation and change it into a familiar one with which we know how to cope. Later on man learns to amuse himself by fooling around with ideas for their own sake. But the basic biological purpose of thinking is to enable a living organism to survive by getting the things it needs and keeping clear of the things that are dangerous. It is a matter of knowing what to do about a situation: does one run forwards in greed or backwards in fear?

Three basic know-all processes

There are three basic processes used by living organisms to know enough about things to react to them properly.

1 Instinct

This is a fixed reaction built into the organism so that a special situation will automatically elicit a special response. The response is pre-wired. It is as direct, automatic and unchanging as the illumination of a room if you switch on the light. The response is built into the organism just as the electric wires are built into a house. No learning is required. Animals show instinct responses to situations which they could not possibly have encountered before. A particular black silhouette moved above naïve nestlings will make them cower in fright because it suggests the shape of a hawk moving through the sky. Exactly the same shape moved backwards has no effect because it looks like a harmless swan. Instincts are precise responses set off by precise situations. Young gulls open their mouths for food as soon as a beak-like shape with a red spot on it appears above them, because this is how the mother gull looks. A piece of wood bearing a red spot will produce the same response. This type of direct response has been beautifully worked out by Tinbergen.

Advantages

1. An instinct response is immediate and perfect and requires no learning at all.

2. An instinct response is predictable and its meaning does not change. This makes it useful for communicating with other animals.

Disadvantages

1. The instinct response is fixed and cannot be adjusted to suit the situation. Nor can it be abolished if the response is inappropriate.

2. The number of fixed inbuilt responses is limited so there is no way of coping with new situations for which there is no ready-made response.

2 Learning

First-hand learning

This is a slow process in which an organism finds a suitable response to a situation by trial and error. A secretary finds out how her boss prefers his letters typed. A circus horse learns how to stand on its hind-legs. A cat learns to find its way home. A tennis player learns how to serve. Learning involves doing something about a situation and then seeing what happens. The outcome may be good, bad or indifferent. If you eat red berries the taste may be very nasty. If the circus horse stands on its hind-legs it gets rewarded with an apple. Gradually one learns to shape the response so it produces only pleasure and no pain. Once it has been shaped in this way the response is elicited by special situations just as an instinct response might be.

Advantages

1. The advantage of learning over instinct is that one can develop responses to *new* situations.

2. Responses can be exactly adjusted to a situation. Bad responses can be improved or abolished.

Disadvantages

1. Learning is very slow as one has to mess around with trial and error. This is especially so with long-range learning where the reward does not come at once but only after a long sequence of responses (so you cannot tell at once whether you are on the right track or not).

2. Direct learning can be dangerous. It would be very dangerous if everyone had to find out about an electric socket for themselves by putting their fingers into it.

Second-hand learning

This is a sort of artificial instinct. It involves acquiring immediate responses to situations without having had to go through the slow trial and error process for oneself. It is passed-on or second-hand learning. It comes from books, TV, school, parents, other people, etc. A child learns that a car is dangerous without having to find out for himself. A

13

student learns that vitamin B_{12} can cure a certain type of anaemia because his medical textbook tells him so. A man learns that an investment is risky because his broker tells him so.

Advantages

1. Second-hand learning is very much quicker and safer than first-hand learning.

2. Second-hand learning can apply in advance to situations which have not yet been met.

3. Second-hand learning can apply to situations which would never be encountered (for instance geography lessons about far-away lands).

4. Second-hand learning can be stored and passed on (books, etc.) so that the total body of learning grows and grows.

5. Lots of different minds (some much better than one's own) can get to work on a situation and produce a much better response than one could by direct first-hand learning.

Disadvantages

1. You depend entirely on the trustworthiness of the source that is passing on the learning. Since you do not encounter the situation directly you can only meet it through the possibly prejudiced eyes of the person who is handing on the learning.

2. The second-hand response is a sort of average response suitable for everybody and not as finely tuned to individual requirements as a response learned at first hand.

3. There may easily be conflicting responses passed on by different sources of second-hand learning (e.g. parents, teachers, pals). This can be confusing.

4. Since reward and punishment are less direct there is not so much keenness to learn as with first-hand learning.

3 Understanding

An instinct is a response fitted to a special situation. The smell of a female moth entices the male moth from miles away. In first- or second-hand learning responses are also fitted to special situations. These become 'familiar' situations because one knows what to do about them. But what about new situations? What about unfamiliar situations which do not have any ready-made responses? A strange woman appears on the doorstep. Immediately you try and put the situation into a familiar category to which you know the response. Is she carrying out some sort of poll? Is she trying to sell you a flag for charity? Has her car broken down? Has she just lost her way? Is she an old acquaintance whose face you have forgotten?

Understanding is the process of changing an unfamiliar process into a familiar one so that you know what to do about it. This changing around takes place in the mind as you go from one idea to another until the unfamiliar situation is seen to resemble or be derived from familiar situations. This going from one idea to another is thinking. Understanding is thinking.

If you see a white sheet flapping in the night it is frightening because it is an unfamiliar situation, but as soon as you can see it as a sheet on a washing-line then you know what to do – nothing. In a foreign restaurant you try and relate the strange words on the menu to words you already know in order to understand what dishes are available. In the end you find that some of the most exotic names refer to very familiar dishes.

Understanding is a very powerful process because it is the means by which man multiplies his knowledge. He can only learn responses to a few special situations but through understanding he converts any number of new situations into already familiar situations and thus knows what to do about them at once (without having to develop a response through first-hand learning or ask for one from second-hand learning).

Advantages

1. Understanding allows one to multiply learning by using old responses in new situations.

2. With understanding you can explain new situations to other people so that they can choose their own responses instead of having to accept second-hand responses blindly.

Disadvantages

1. Understanding is limited by the available old responses (or ideas) with which to explain the new situations.

2. In trying to understand a new unfamiliar situation in terms of old ideas one may leave out a lot or distort the actual situation to make it fit the available ideas.

3. It is usually possible to understand an unfamiliar situation in several alternative ways but one is apt to settle on the first way and believe this to be the only possible way.

4. Different people may understand the same situation in quite different ways and act accordingly.

Thinking in practice

In practice modern man does not use instinct very much. Nor does he have much time for direct first-hand learning. He depends nearly all the time on passed-on second-hand learning and on understanding. His basic knowledge and ideas come from the second-hand learning that is deliberately passed on to him in education or which he picks up through interest or accident. He then uses his understanding to break down new unfamiliar situations into familiar parts so that he can apply his basic knowledge.

Why bother?

Why should man bother to try and understand things?

1. In order to react suitably: avoid, ignore, alter, enjoy, use, examine, etc.

2. In order to bring about effects: cure disease, produce better crops, overcome poverty, fly faster than sound, prevent crime, win yacht races, etc.

3. In order to tell what is going to happen later: to a child with a high temperature, to the stock-market, to the weather, to the polluted environment, etc.

4. Curiosity.

Basic thinking process

The change from unknown to known is understanding, and the way this change comes about is thinking. It may be a matter of understanding what something is or it may be a matter of understanding how to bring about some effect. Understanding is finding out what to do. This finding out is thinking.

Understanding is thinking.

The Black Cylinder Experiment

Imagine a tall black cylinder standing on a white table in front of you. No one is near the table and there is nothing on the table except the cylinder which stands stark and alone. About twenty minutes pass. Suddenly, without warning, the cylinder falls over with a crash. Why? No one has gone near it. Nothing has been seen to happen. There is no sound except the crash of the falling cylinder. You are asked to try and understand what has happened and to write down your explanation on a card. But you have only ten minutes in which to think of an explanation – and you are not allowed to examine the cylinder in any way.

Experimental subjects

The experiment was carried out on a number of different occasions. Altogether one thousand people took part. These people came from a wide variety of backgrounds: university lecturers, research scientists (university), research scientists (industry), doctors, senior management executives, advertising executives, advertising copywriters, engineering students, psychology students, arts students (university), fine arts students (art college), architecture students, secondary school teachers, primary school teachers, student teachers (training college).

Relevance

The black cylinder experiment was deliberately kept simple so that the thinking processes involved in trying to understand the phenomenon could be easily analysed. What relevance does this experiment have to everyday thinking? There are the following points which are common both to everyday thinking and to the black cylinder experiment:

1. Not enough information is given.
2. There is no opportunity to collect the data one needs.
3. Trial and error experimentation is not possible.
4. There is no way of checking whether an idea is right or wrong.
5. It is not a closed situation in which one can prove that one is right.
6. There may be several different explanations.
7. One is dealing with vague ideas and not with precise numbers which can be put through a mathematical formula.
8. It is not so much a matter of checking ideas but of thinking of them first.
9. In spite of the inadequate information one is required to come to a definite conclusion.
10. There is no one to ask.

Out of the thousand people who took part in the experiment only three wrote on their cards: 'I do not care.' This is a perfectly valid response for no one is obliged to understand anything. If you do not care to understand something then you must borrow an explanation from someone else or do without one.

Process not content

In looking at thinking the usual difficulty is to separate the thinking process from what is being thought about. The atomic physicist may be thinking in terms of quarks and neutrinos. The housewife may be thinking of the price of mutton. But the actual thinking process may be the same. This thinking process is determined by the nature of mind itself. There is no switch that can be flipped as one moves from trivial matters to more serious ones. It is the same thinking engine that is working. The thinking behaviour shown in the black cylinder experiment is determined by the characteristics of the same mind which has to deal with such things as politics and passion and peeling potatoes.

Raw thinking

The experimental subjects were at a disadvantage because they had insufficient data, insufficient chance to examine the cylinder and insufficient time to think up an explanation. The intended result of this insufficient 'cooking' was raw thinking. Given enough time and information the explanations would have been much better. There would have been a careful process of analysis and checking until everything either seemed right or was rejected. From the perfection of the result it would have been impossible to tell anything about the process behind it. But in a hurriedly constructed building the joints, cracks and method of construction are much easier to see.

Results

Some of the results confirm what one might have expected. Others are quite contrary to expectation. The main use of the results is that they provide a tangible framework for identifying the basic features of thinking: the four ways to be right; the five ways to be wrong; the five ways to understand; and such things as humour, creativity, imagination and attention. These are the stuff of everyday thinking. If one can learn to look at these aspects of thinking objectively then one can start to do something about them. The black cylinder experiment provides a magnifying glass with which to look at thinking.

The Five Ways to Understand

How do you explain an event you cannot understand? It may
be an eclipse, it may be a strange illness in which a person falls
to the ground in a sudden fit, it may be the failure of a crop, it
may be the way young people take to drugs, it may be the way
a solid black cylinder falls over. In everyday thinking five
levels of understanding are used to explain such things to
oneself or to others.

L-1 Simple description

'It fell.'
'The black cylinder suddenly fell over.'
'It changed position suddenly.'
'Fell over on its side.'
'The tube fell over.'
'Changed from a vertical to a horizontal position.'

These explanations of why the black cylinder fell over are
simple descriptions of what happened. A description is the
simplest possible level of explanation. You simply say what
you saw happening. The only way to say less would be to say
nothing at all.

Well over 20 per cent of those taking part in the experiment
used simple descriptions. But do these simple descriptions

actually tell us anything at all? Do they not just say: 'The black cylinder fell over because it fell over'? At first sight it would seem that this sort of circularity is no better than saying nothing at all. But if you look more closely you can see that these simple descriptions do actually say quite a lot. They are true explanations because they commit the viewer to a definite point of view. In order to realize what these descriptions do say you need to consider not their content but *what they leave out*.

If I had pulled the tube over by a nylon thread which was so fine that it was invisible to most of the viewers then those who could not see the thread would write as above:

'The tube fell over.'

But those who did see the thread would write:

'The tube was pulled over by the lecturer.'

Impossible to say nothing

It is impossible to say nothing at all if one says something. This important point arises directly from the validity of simple description as a type of understanding. The simple descriptions which explained that the cylinder 'fell over' all imply that this falling over was to do with the cylinder itself. This excludes the idea of the cylinder being 'knocked over' as suggested by many other people in the course of the experiment:

'... blown over by the wind.'

'... shot at by an accomplice in the audience.'

'... table was tilted.'

'... table was shaken.'

'... lecturer walked over when no one was looking and knocked it over.'

'... pulled over by invisible wire.'

The person putting forward the simple description may not have *meant* to exclude all these possibilities but in committing himself to a description he is already making a choice of explanation. Any description which does not include all possibilities is a commitment to those it does include. In practice descriptions never do include all possibilities, for the person making the description is not describing the *actual situation itself* but the *way he sees it.*

Pass it on

The person offering the simple description may keep his options open by being prepared to go back to the actual situation and describe it in another way. But once he has passed his description on to someone else (as a journalist might pass on a description) then the receiver is committed to that point of view since *he* does not have the real situation itself to examine.

I would certainly accept the simple statement, 'It fell over,' as a valid first-level explanation of what happened.

L–2 Porridge words

'Cylinder had time controlled "knocking over device".'
'Device in tube caused it to unbalance.'
'Device inside to make it fall over.'
'Timing device which re-distributes balance.'
'It was unbalanced by a time device of some kind devised for this purpose.'
'The cylinder had a mechanism to make it fall over after a certain time.'
'The cylinder fell due to some mechanism putting it off balance.'
'The switch eventually released something inside the object which disturbed the balance and so it fell over.'
'The black thing contained a mechanism to make it fall over.'

23

Porridge words indicate definite ideas but when you go to examine the ideas you find that like porridge they have no form, no shape, and there is no definite meaning that can be grasped. Yet the ideas do exist and one reacts to them in a real way. The French have succeeded in reducing traffic accidents by putting plywood silhouettes of policemen and police cars beside the roads. What matters is not the emptiness behind the image but the surface appearance to which drivers react. In the same way porridge words though empty of meaning do have a real and useful effect.

If anything at all happens you can say that there is a 'mechanism' for making it happen. Thus to say that there is a mechanism or 'device' to make the cylinder fall over is not really different from saying, 'The cylinder fell over.' For instance the following explanation may seem to be a rather elaborate way of saying nothing at all:

'Black cylinder has some mechanism which once set takes a given time to destroy the equilibrium which enables the cylinder to remain upright. The cylinder fell when the vertical equilibrium was destroyed by the mechanism.'

While waiting at an airport to catch a flight you often hear announcements that certain flights have been delayed for 'operational reasons'. Since operational reasons could include everything from the lateness of the incoming plane to a bomb scare the announcement really says no more than that the flight has been delayed 'because it has been delayed.' But if you made that sort of announcement the passengers would riot.

Very useful meaningless words

Porridge-word explanation (L–2) is much more specific than simple description (L–1). A definite reason is now given instead of just a simple description. The reason is stated as follows:

'knocking over device'
'device'
'timing device'
'mechanism'
'something'

Instead of just saying, 'The cylinder fell over,' the explanation reveals that the cylinder fell over 'due to *something*'. This something may be called a 'something' or it may be given the more impressive name of 'mechanism' or 'device'. Further elaboration gives: 'a knocking over device'; 'a device devised to knock the cylinder over'; 'a timing device'.

The use of such porridge words is *not* a cheat. It is not a way of seeming to say a lot without actually saying anything. The use of meaningless porridge words is a hugely important part of human thinking. Because man is able to use these meaningless words which say nothing he is able to think more effectively than animals. To be useful these words *must* be blurred, formless and porridge-like. You can push out such a porridge word ahead of you and then you have something to work towards. This very important process is described more fully in a later section.

L–3 Give it a name

'With God all things are possible.'
'By magic.'
'I don't understand it therefore it is magic.'
'Some magical process.'
'Mirrors? Weights and pulleys? Magic!'

'It fell over – reason gravity.'
'Some clockwork or gravity device in the black cylinder

created an imbalance after a period of time causing it to topple.'

'The black cylinder fell over because electrical charge knocked it over.'

'Due to an electrical current.'

'Electrical impulse operating from a battery made the black tower topple.'

'Electric magnet.'

'Black thing received a jolt from electric battery.'

'Equilibrium inside changed due to shocks.'

Magic and magnets

This third level of understanding involves identifying and naming the process involved. Instead of just using a porridge word like 'device' the actual mechanism is named: 'God', 'magic', 'gravity', 'electricity'. The details of how the mechanism brings about the observed effect are not given. Nor are such details necessary, for with God and magic all things are possible. Those who put down God or magic as explanations were presumably not being serious, but it is a level of understanding that is much used to explain strange happenings. In one of the examples given above, magic refers to 'stage magic'. As everyone knows, a stage magician can do the most impossible things using mirrors and pulleys. To explain the situation there is no need to give functional details. It is enough to name the mechanism as stage magic or real magic or God.

Naming the mechanism is a very big step forward from simply saying 'a device'. In fact it is such a big step forward that it really provides a full explanation. As soon as you can name a mechanism you know what to do about it and knowing what to do about it is the only reason you want to understand something in the first place. By identifying the mechanism as magic you know that there is nothing that can be done about it or that you have to find some more powerful counter-magic. In either case naming the mechanism *relieves* one of the necessity of looking further for an explanation.

Modern magic

Magic is a mysterious force which can make things happen, though exactly how it does so remains obscure. 'Gravity' is a modern name which we give to an equally mysterious force. We know its effects but we do not know how it works.

The most modern form of magic is electricity. It is sufficient explanation to say that something happens 'due to an electrical current'. Electricity is all-powerful. Electricity can be made to do anything. As with magic, you do not have to know the details in order to control it – by flicking a switch or pulling out a plug. But to control a mechanism you do have to identify it first.

Minor magic

God, magic, electricity and gravity are major magic and they can accomplish most things. Many more explanations made use of minor magic. This minor magic consisted of specific named mechanisms like 'magnets', 'springs', 'heat', etc. No details were given to show how these mechanisms were involved in the fall of the black cylinder. It was enough to name the mechanisms since they were obviously capable of bringing about this sort of effect.

'Build-up of heat in cylinder.'
'Spring inside knocks it over.'
'Timing device with spring altered balance.'
'Black object – some kind of spring device.'
'Timed spring mechanism.'
'Magnetic effect.'
'Pulled over by a magnet.'

The three most used minor-magic mechanisms were:

27

springs, magnets, heat. Of those who gave specific explanations for the fall of the cylinder the following percentages used these elements of minor magic:

springs	12·8%
magnets	11·6%
heat	11·4%

It is interesting to note that in children's drawings there is always a great use of springs and magnets to bring about desired effects. Springs and magnets, like God and magic, can be made to do just about anything.

Names mean a lot

As soon as you can name the mechanism involved the unfamiliar situation is at once understood. You can rush out and hit the stone field-gods over the head if the crops are bad; you can switch off the electric current if the machine runs amok; you can start by getting a magnet or a spring if you want to make a black cylinder topple over. As soon as you can name the mechanism as Communism, Fascism, Papism, Racism, Imperialism, Establishment, Government, Radicals, Them, then you know what to do about things – or that you need look no further for an explanation.

L–4 The way it works

'Overbalanced due to a slow shifting of contents.'

'Change of balance due to rising object in the tube.'

'Because of its upright position a weight inside it moved upwards and made it overbalance.'

'Something at the bottom rose up to make it top-heavy . . . overbalanced.'

'Cylinder fell due to becoming top-heavy.'

'The centre of gravity of the cylinder was moved so as to be no longer over the base.'

'Centre of gravity moved past critical point of previous equilibrium.'

'Cylinder toppled over due to change in centre of gravity.'

'Centre of gravity shifted.'

'One section of the base was made of a "plastic" material that sagged (crept) until cylinder became unstable.'

'False base which snaps up on one side causing cylinder to tip and fall.'

'Cylinder – edge over which it fell made of slowly compressionable material.'

'Something came out of bottom of black tube at one side and made it overbalance.'

Cause and effect

The fall of the black cylinder is a definite happening. One can explain a happening by showing how it follows directly from something that happened just before. What happened just before is the *cause*: 'weight inside cylinder moving upwards'; 'change in centre of gravity'; 'slowly compressed edge'; 'something coming out of the bottom of the tube', etc. What happens next is the *effect*: 'cylinder falls over'. Cause and effect is no more than chopping a chain of happenings at some convenient point and calling what goes before the chop 'cause' and what comes after it 'effect'.

This fourth level of understanding shows how the visible happening is really the outcome of another happening which is invisible. Thus one explains the unfamiliar situation by moving backwards along the chain of happenings until one finds a happening which is familiar. A shift of contents, a change in the centre of gravity, a pin coming out of the base are all much less strange than a cylinder toppling over. By looking at the strange fall of the cylinder in terms of these familiar processes one is explaining the way it works.

At this level of explanation the actual details of the process are not given. We are not told how the centre of gravity was changed or what rose up the tube. There is simply a *general* description of the way it works. The emphasis is on what happens not on the bits and pieces that make it happen. The emphasis is on the process not on how it is carried out. Thus a painter would be described as 'climbing up to paint the ceiling'. Whether the painter used a step-ladder or put a chair on a table would not be specified. This approach is almost exactly opposite to the approach used in the third level of explanation. At that level the mechanism was specifically named but the actual way it worked was not described. We are told that magnets or springs are somehow used to make the cylinder fall over. At this fourth level of explanation the way things work is described but no specific mechanism is named. We are told that a weight rises up the cylinder but we are not told whether the weight is raised by a magnet or spring or electric motor.

Name or process

In practice it is often possible to move from an understanding of the way something works to giving a name to the process. Alternatively if one can give a name to the mechanism one often has some idea of the way it works. You can diagnose a disease as dysentery and then go on to consider the bacterial infection and the loss of fluid from the body. Or you may look at the loss of fluid and evidence of infection and then go on to use the name 'dysentery'.

The advantage of the naming level of understanding is that it is much easier to identify a mechanism than to show exactly how it works. It is easier to call something magic than to show how magic works. This is an advantage because it enables you to go ahead and *do something* without having to wait until you have figured out the way it works. But this can be a disadvantage for you may rest content with the name of the mechanism instead of going on to find out the way it works. If you do really want to find out the way something works it is much better to start with the process type of understanding and leave names until the end.

Follows on

In trying to understand the way something works one is trying to find causes for the observed effects. As suggested above this is equivalent to taking a step backwards in time to show that the unfamiliar happening follows on directly from a familiar happening. This is much the best way of looking at cause and effect since it includes the whole scene. If one tries to isolate a specific cause one is apt to leave out other necessary factors. This happened very often in the black cylinder experiment and is discussed in the mistakes section further on.

L–5 Full details

'You kicked the desk.'

'An accomplice hiding behind the desk knocked it over while we were preoccupied.'

'Someone shot it down from the window on the right.'

'Vibrations of overhead projector together with fans and breeze from window acting on a barely stable situation.'

'The tube was unstable but was stuck to the table bv adhesive which eventually gave way.'

'Concealed clockwork mouse with suction pad feet climbs up tube which becomes top-heavy and falls over. Clockwork mechanism is silent.'

(Detailed drawings are shown on page 33.)

This fifth level of understanding is the most detailed level to which you can go. It is like providing blue-prints or working models so that someone can follow exactly what has happened to the black cylinder. At this level most of the explanations were in fact put in the form of a drawing. Instead of just being told that something works 'by electricity' you are shown a torch battery connected by wires and a switch to a motor which rotates a spiral shaft to raise a weight to the top of the cylinder.

Some of the drawings were quite complicated, but to be detailed an explanation does not have to be complicated. For instance the explanation, 'You kicked the desk,' is just as much a detailed explanation as the drawing showing lead shot trickling on to a balloon in the base (page 33). The mechanism itself may be complicated or simple – the explanation provides details of whatever mechanism is involved.

How full are full details?

It is obviously never possible to give complete details in an absolute sense. For instance what are the internal changes in the metal of a spring that give it springiness? In an explanation one can go on offering more and more detail without ever being able to say that the full details (in an absolute sense) have been given. *In practice* one stops at that fullness of detail which makes it unnecessary for anyone to ask why or how. At this point an unfamiliar situation has become changed into a familiar one. The paradox is that if you go beyond practical detail to further detail the situation may become unfamiliar again. Thus the springiness of a spring is familiar enough but to go further and discuss the metallurgy of a spring would make the explanation less understandable.

Combination of third and fourth levels

The fifth level of understanding is a combination of the third and fourth levels. As in the fourth level the explanation describes the way things work but it goes further in specifying

Other solid

Ice

Hole

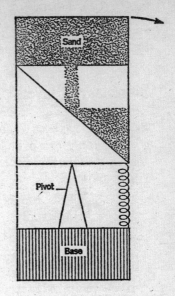

Sand

Pivot

Base

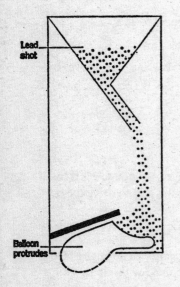

Lead shot

Balloon protrudes

Weight shoots across when catch gives way

and naming the bits and pieces that are actually involved. Further than that it is impossible to go.

Summary of levels of understanding

Explanation has been regarded throughout this section as the communicable form of understanding. Understanding is personal and subjective. Explanation makes this understanding visible to others.

L–1 Simple description
L–2 Porridge words
L–3 Give it a name
L–4 The way it works
L–5 Full details

If you were asked to explain how a car worked the five levels of explanation might go roughly as follows:

Simple description

'A car goes along the road and people sit in it.'

Porridge words

'There is a mechanism which makes the car move by itself.'

Give it a name

'The car is driven by petrol.'

The way it works

'Energy provided by expanding gases in the engine is transmitted to the wheels to turn them round and so drive the car forward.'

Full details

'Petrol carried in a refillable tank is pumped through a feed-pipe to the carburettor where it is mixed with air by being drawn through a fine nozzle. The resulting explosive mixture is admitted to the top end of the cylinder at the right point in the engine cycle by the opening of a valve activated by a cam driven off the crankshaft of the engine. The mixture is then compressed by the rising piston and ignited by a high voltage discharging as a spark across the points of a spark plug...etc.'

Levels used everywhere

The five levels of understanding outlined here are not only used in explanations but in all manner of thinking, talking or arguing about a subject. Thus one person may describe a riot simply in terms of what he saw; a second person will talk about 'crowd psychology'; a third person will name the mechanism as Communist agitation; a fourth person will talk about the underlying processes and background to the riot; and a fifth person will try and supply full details. These same levels of understanding also provide the basis for action and for decision.

It may seem a long way from the simplicity of the black cylinder experiment to the complexity of a riot but one is dealing not with cylinders or riots but with the basic habits of the mind.

It is impossible to say nothing at all if one says something.

It is only because man is able to use these meaningless words which say nothing that he is able to think more effectively than animals.

As soon as you can name a mechanism you know what to do about it and knowing what to do about it is the only reason you want to understand something in the first place.

In practice one stops at that fullness of detail which makes it unnecessary for anyone to ask why or how.

The paradox is that if you go beyond practical detail to further detail the situation may become unfamiliar again.

4

The Use of Understanding

How much detail

1,000 people tried to understand the fall of the black cylinder.
325 (32·5 per cent) of them offered a first- (L–1) or second-
(L–2) level explanation. Was this because they *could not* proceed to a deeper level? Or because they did not have enough
time? Or because they felt that this level of explanation was
quite *good enough*?

What level of understanding does one choose? Does one
go as deep as one can? Or does one stop as soon as one reaches
a level which allows one to act? Or does one first go as deep as
possible and then come back to a more practical level?

Scientific analysis

In looking at the five levels of explanation one is apt to feel
that the deeper one can go the better it must be. Level five
seems better than level four and in turn four seems better
than level three. This is the scientific tradition which insists
that things must be explained *as fully as possible*. So one proceeds down to the finest detail and then tries to push even
further by means of experiment and observation. The search
for the fullest details is an end in itself – it is not a question of
getting enough detail for action. 'The fertilized or un-
fertilized ovum of a hen encased with a food sac in a hard
calcerous shell shaped in an ellipsoidal fashion which makes it

resistant to crush deformation (but not to shock impact), is placed in water at 100° centigrade (at sea-level) for three minutes during which time the albumen protein part of the egg is coagulated and . . .' This is the full-detail attitude. From this attitude have come man's greatest scientific and technological achievements. But in ordinary practical thinking explanation and understanding are rather different: 'Put the pan on the fire and when you see the water bubbling put in the egg. Take it out again after three minutes.'

Everyday thinking

In scientific analysis there is much data and little action, whereas in everyday thinking there is much action but little data. Action is the main purpose of everyday thinking. It is not a matter of accumulating as much knowledge as possible but of coming up with just enough knowledge to tell you what to do next.

A scientist may choose to spend his life narrowly focused on the genetic structure of a gnat's wing. Scientific inquiry can choose to focus on a tiny field of interest but everyday thinking has to cope with a variety of situations which are not chosen but thrust at it. Usually there is very little data available. Everyday thinking has to deal with vague subjects like human behaviour, politics and economics. Even when there is good data available it may be difficult to get hold of in time for action.

If everyday thinking followed the habits of scientific inquiry, life would be impossible for no one would be able to take any practical action. In everyday thinking the aim of understanding is quite different from what it is in scientific inquiry. Instead of the automatic search for the most detailed level of explanation, there is a search for the simplest level of explanation that allows one to get on and do something. As soon as it allows one to do something about the situation then an explanation is detailed enough. A husband comes home in the evening and is irritable and bad-tempered. His wife does not know how to cope with him – until she learns that he lost his brief-case on the train.

Doing something

An explanation is detailed enough if it allows one to:

1. Decide that the situation is not worth bothering about and can be ignored (e.g. the black cylinder).
2. Decide that the situation is important but requires no further action at the moment (e.g. a fall in stock-market prices).
3. Decide that the situation is dangerous and ought to be avoided (e.g. mixing radial and cross-ply tyres on your car).
4. Decide that the situation is good and should be enjoyed (e.g. a holiday travel bargain).
5. Decide on a *particular* response to a *particular* situation (e.g. a doctor choosing penicillin to treat pneumonia).
6. Decide that one needs a more detailed explanation (e.g. taking a look at the thinking process).

None of these require an immediate full-detail explanation. An explanation at any of the other levels can enable one to do something – to move on. What one goes on to do may of course involve working up more details for a fifth-level explanation. But that would only happen some of the time.

Need and use

Consider a steep valley that has to be crossed. If you are on foot and in a hurry you could run across the flimsy bridge that spans the top of the valley. If you have a car you would use the shorter and hence stronger bridge that is set lower down the valley wall. If you had a truck you would want to use an even shorter and stronger bridge set nearer to the valley floor. If you wanted absolute safety and reliability you would descend to the valley floor, cross it and climb up the other side. These bridges of different strength set at different levels correspond to levels of understanding. You use the bridge or level that is strong enough for your purpose. You do not need to descend to the valley floor every time you want to cross any more than you need to know the molecular structure of albumen in order to boil an egg. If you are in a hurry the long flimsy bridge across the top of the valley might be more practical.

Detail danger

Although the most detailed level of explanation may not be necessary on all occasions, is it not better to strive for it whenever possible? One does feel that one should really be working at level five if only one could. One admires detailed explanations and apologizes for the superficiality of lesser levels of explanation. It must make more sense to understand about crop diseases and so treat them than to ascribe crop failure to the displeasure of the stone field-gods.

On the other hand there can be a danger in too much detail. In analysing the results of the black cylinder experiment I soon found that it was impossible to count how many explanations would work and how many would not. This was easy enough with the detailed explanations and drawings but impossible at other levels where a general statement could include a correct explanation even if the viewer could not actually think of one. 'The cylinder contains a device to make it fall over': is that right or wrong? As politicians, doctors, astrologers and forecasters well know, one reduces the risk of being wrong by sticking to a general level of explanation, for by committing oneself to detail one increases the risk of error. This may seem a cowardly attitude. But if you have to choose a suitable action it is better to base it on a general explanation which is unlikely to be wrong than a detailed explanation which might well be wrong. In science, however, the whole

39

aim is to commit yourself to enough detail to prove yourself wrong because that is the method by which you change your ideas into better ones.

Even in science the attempt to provide detailed explanations can do more harm than good when there is not enough data to throw out the explanation. There is a strong tendency in human thinking to produce immensely detailed systems which are validated only by the tidy way the pieces fit together. The history of science is full of the detailed explanations of alchemy, astrology, phrenology, etc. The history of medicine and psychology is particularly full of detailed explanations which have impeded progress much more than they have helped it. If you have only a vague explanation then you try and improve it and are open to new ideas. If you have a detailed and apparently complete explanation all you want is to preserve and defend it.

Usefulness is what matters

It would be quite wrong to suggest that general explanations were better than detailed ones. But it would be just as wrong to claim that detailed explanations were automatically better than general ones. What really matters is the usefulness of the explanation. Often detail adds no more usefulness – only a false appearance of validity. The important thing about explanation is where it gets one. And it may be easier to move forward from a general idea than from a detailed idea from which one would first have to retreat. The snag is that one may be more reluctant to move at all from a general idea since there would seem less need to change it.

Black boxes

How does a car work? It works 'by switching on the ignition'. That is all most people know about cars. They know that there is an engine somewhere (you don't even have to know whether it is in the front or in the back) and gears and things but you do not have to know how such things work in order to use a car. You just get in and switch on and you are able to use the car as effectively as someone who knows all about petrol engines and carburettors and fuel injection.

To most people the car is a 'black box'. You know how to use it but you do not know what goes on inside it. The name 'black box' indicates that you cannot see what is happening inside. All you need to know about a black box is that if you do certain things (like switching on the ignition) then certain other things will happen (like the car starting). You do not need to know what happens in between. To make a telephone call you do not need to know about microphones, induction coils, relay banks, repeaters, etc. To switch on a TV set and watch a cowboy film you do not need to know about cathode-ray tubes, phosphors, saw-tooth signals, thyristors, etc. All you need to know about a vacuum-cleaner is that you press a button and it starts to clean.

Press the right button

By far the most striking feature in children's designs in the five- to eight-year age group is the way they use press-button control. Every machine no matter how primitive is carefully supplied with an 'on' button to make it go and an 'off' button to stop it. The buttons do not control the internal works. The buttons *are* the works.

If a certain effect is to be produced then you provide a special button to press. 'You press the right button and everything happens.' In one design by a six-year-old for a postman's bicycle there were three buttons: the first button provided a ready-made cup of hot tea; the second button ensured that the bicycle moved and steered itself while the postman read a comic (a sort of automatic pilot); and the third button materialized an instant slave who would run and drop the letters into letter-boxes. The three buttons were arrayed on the handle-bars. In a design for a 'fun-machine' one child provided a neat little control panel that could be worn on the wrist like a watch. On this panel were a number of tiny buttons which you pressed in order to get 'fun' things. If you pressed the right button you could have a chocolate cake. If you pressed the right button you could have a nurse's kit. If you pressed the right button you could have circus animals – 'and a lion'.

This press-button idiom is the direct result of growing up in an electric/electronic age. All you have is a box and you press the right button and you get the effect you want. This press-button idiom replaces the old cause and effect idiom in which you watched how things happened. In the cause and effect idiom if you wanted to wash clothes you slopped them around in a tub; if you wanted to haul bricks up to the top of a building you used rope and pulley. In the press-button idiom you use a washing machine or a lift and simply press the right button in each case. The change-over from the cause and effect idiom to the press-button idiom may well be the most important cultural change in thinking that has happened for many hundreds of years.

Spells and special gods

In a way the press-button idiom is a return to the days of spells and special gods. If you wanted to produce a certain effect what you had to do was to 'trigger it off' with the right spell or ju-ju. If you wanted to make it rain you pressed the right button. If you wanted to make your enemy sick you pressed the right button. The spell or ju-ju bore no more understandable a relation to the effect produced than does pressing a button to a TV picture. Instead of an observable chain of cause and effect it all happens in a mysterious way. The process has become one of *identification*. Instead of trying to *make* things happen one finds the right button (or spell or ju-ju) and sets things in motion. As suggested earlier electricity is the modern magic which is got going by pressing the right button.

More primitive but more advanced

This press-button idiom may seem more primitive as it is a return to the days of 'magic'. Yet in another way it is an advance to a *more sophisticated* way of looking at things. An increasing interest in the organization of complex systems has replaced the static nineteenth-century approach to science. This is partly the result of increased interest in living organisms which are complex systems that cannot be taken apart as one might take apart a steam-engine. If you pile three books one on top of another then there are three books piled one on top of another until you take them away again. This is the old cause and effect idiom – the static approach. In complex systems things are going on all the time. It is not so much a matter of making things happen but of finding the right way of influencing things in order to trigger off some effect. This is the dynamic approach. The effect produced is not the obvious result of what you do but depends on the black box working of the system itself, just as a TV picture depends on the internal workings of the TV set and is only triggered off by your pressing the right button. When a doctor uses the antibiotic tetracycline to kill germs it is not really the equivalent of knocking each germ on the head with a little hammer as it would be if he had used strong disinfectant. The antibiotic triggers off certain changes in the germ itself which make it unable to produce more germs. Then the body's own defence system kills off the germs. So with the antibiotic one is really making use of both the germ's 'system' and the body's 'system'.

In medicine and biology one recognizes the existence of complex systems and is always looking for the right button to trigger off the effects one wants. Occasionally one understands the whole mechanism involved but most of the time one finds useful buttons to press without really knowing what is the actual mechanism that is being started up. Aspirin is one of the most useful and effective of all drugs and its consumption is measured in tons. And yet we have no idea how aspirin actually works. The use of aspirin is still rather like that postman's bicycle where you press a button and a ready-made cup of tea appears. It is this shift towards the use of complex systems by finding and pressing the right button that is more advanced than the crude cause and effect manipulation of the past. For instance today a few words carefully chosen for their media-triggering effect can be more effective in influencing people's thinking than such crude measures as concentration camps or burnings at the stake.

Automation age

As factory machinery, or indeed the machinery of living, gets more and more complicated, it is suggested that there will come a time when the majority of people will not be clever enough to do anything. This danger will be avoided by the switch-over to the press-button idiom. No matter how complex the machine is all you have to do is press the right button. After all a car is really a very complicated piece of machinery. Yet it does not require a genius or an engineer to drive a car.

Ignorance tools

Some people feel that a black box is really just another word for ignorance. It is. But it makes it possible to *use* ignorance in an effective way instead of being held up by it. The car engineer might look down his nose at the fluffy blonde who regards the car as a magic black box which is worked by turning the ignition key.

But the engineer is himself using black boxes in exactly

44

the same way. Does he know all there is to know about the physical chemistry of exploding petrol or just enough to *use* this explosion in a black box fashion? Does he know all there is to know about the surface physics of lubricants or does he just use them in a black box fashion as lubricants which have certain properties? Does he know all there is to know about the metallurgy of gear wheels or just use the gear wheels made available to him as black boxes?

No matter how far back one pushes understanding one always comes to black boxes in the end. This is because it is easier to notice an effect than to understand how it is produced. The Saracens were using nitrogen to improve the quality of steel in their sword blades by heating them up and then plunging them into the body of a slave long before the process of making special steel by using nitrogen was worked out.

Science is full of black boxes. Gravity is a very good example of a black box. We know its effects, how to calculate it, and how to use it with enough precision to send men around the moon. But we do not really understand it. 'Magnetism' is another black box. So is the idea of an 'electron' or for that matter 'light' itself. One of the most fundamental processes of the human body is the way sodium is pumped out of cells into the fluid which bathes them. The whole activity of the brain and nervous system depends on this action. But we know very little about it. Sodium appears to move in a direction contrary to its natural 'flow'. So we simply say there must be a sodium 'pump' because we use a pump to make water move against its natural flow. This is exactly the same as saying, 'There is a mechanism to make the cylinder fall over.'

Leap-frog

Black boxes are extremely useful. Life (and science) would be impossible without them. They are useful because they allow

45

us to move on both in thinking and in action. There would not be many cars on the road if every driver had to know all there was to know about petrol engines and transmissions. TV advertising would hardly be effective if the only TV watchers were those who knew enough about their sets to be able to make them themselves.

Black boxes enable us to use an effect without actually knowing the details of how it is produced. They allow us to get on with things in spite of ignorance. All you need to know is how to trigger off the effect in a reliable manner. So you learn the right button to press and then you can 'leap-frog' over all the details in between and *use* the effect you want.

To use a black box one has first to recognize it in order to know which is the right button to press. Once you can identify the situation then you know what to do to bring about the effect you want. That is why names are so important because they are the chief means of identification.

The use of black boxes corresponds to both the second and third levels of understanding. You can call a TV set a TV set and that explains how it works (L–3, give it a name). Or you can say that there is a 'mechanism' to produce pictures (L–2, porridge words).

Named-ideas and bundle-ideas

A bundle-idea is when two or more ideas are put together into a bundle which is used as such. 'A device to tell time' is a bundle-idea. So is 'the political system in which people elect their government'. If a bundle of ideas are used together often enough they get a name. The device to tell time becomes a 'clock' and the political system becomes 'democracy'. Once it has acquired a name the bundle of ideas becomes permanent. A named-idea is simply a bundle-idea which has become permanent through being given a name. Thus 'clock',

46

'cat', 'mouse', 'love', 'vibration', 'movement', etc., are all named-ideas. Named-ideas are very useful in thinking. It might be difficult to explain to someone who did not have the named-idea 'golf' what highly paid business executives were doing walking erratically about a long, grass meadow in pursuit of a small white ball which they seemed to dislike. If we did not have the named-idea 'government' it might be difficult to think about politics. After all there are a lot of things we should be thinking about but cannot because we have not yet developed named-ideas for them.

Contents

The main advantage of a bundle-idea is that it is put together and pulled apart very easily. A bundle-idea contains only what is put into that bundle at the moment. But a named-idea is a permanent bundle of ideas. Over time one may add further ideas to the original collection but it is very difficult to throw out ideas which are there already. Thus a person who starts out with the idea that capitalists are exploiters may add the idea that they are efficient but is unlikely to start regarding them as social providers.

Movement

Thinking is the process of moving from one idea to another. The use of named-ideas and bundle-ideas automatically generates movement as the mind moves from one to the other. Children dressing up for a fancy-dress party pull pieces of old clothing out of the dressing-up box. One child puts on a certain collection of clothes, whereupon another child says, 'Oh, you look like a gypsy,' (or an Arab sheikh or a pirate). The bundle of clothes has come together to give *a definite name*. Another child may start out with the idea of dressing up as an Arab sheikh and so collect sheets and things which are part of the bundle that makes up the idea of an Arab sheikh. One child has gone from a bundle-idea to a named-idea, the other has gone from a named-idea to a bundle-idea.

This automatic movement can be seen if one starts off with the bundle-idea 'something that moves predictably with the passage of time'. From this one moves to the named-idea of a 'clock'. From this named-idea one moves to the bundle-idea underlying the name a 'device for measuring time'. From this bundle-idea one can move again to a new named-idea 'an egg-timer'. Then on to the underlying bundle-idea 'two containers with sand shifting slowly from one to the other'. At this point one has arrived at a bundle-idea which could explain the fall of the black cylinder. If one wanted one could go further and take the named-idea 'sand' and move to the bundle-idea a 'collection of small particles which are quite heavy'. From this one might move to the named-idea of 'lead-shot' as was suggested in some of the explanations.

When one moves from the named-idea to the underlying bundle-idea this bundle does not have to contain the whole collection of ideas that go to make up the named-idea but only some of them. One can move from the named-idea of 'magnets' to 'an effect at a distance' without having to list all the properties of magnets.

Requirements

In trying to understand a strange situation you can list all the things you notice about it and put them together as a bundle-idea. For instance in the case of the black cylinder the list of 'requirements' might read as follows:

'something which acts after a period of time'
'silent'
'acts suddenly'
'small enough to go into cylinder'
'something to do with a shift of weight'

The hope is that by building up a bundle-idea in this way

you can suddenly *snap* into a named-idea which fits the bundle that has been collected.

Requiron

The list of requirements are really the bundle-idea underlying the named-idea which has not yet been found. Instead of saying: 'That which we are looking for', one can use the much more convenient word 'requiron'. The *requiron* is a temporary named-word to cover the bundle of requirements.

So one could say: 'The requiron must act suddenly, silently and entirely within the cylinder.'

In the case of the black cylinder you could use the word 'mechanism' all along but in other situations 'requiron' could be more convenient: 'The requiron arrived here yesterday between the hours of six and eight in the morning – and probably by car' (a detective discussing a case).

Modification

It would be unusual to list all the requirements at the beginning. Most of the time one starts off with a few, gets to a named-idea, then adds further requirements to modify the named-idea and so gets to another one. A sequence might go something as follows:

'Cylinder was knocked over by something which moved by itself inside.'
'An animal.'
'An animal small enough to fit into the cylinder.'
'A mouse.'
'A mouse that would work in a predictable way.'
'A clockwork mouse.'
'A clockwork mouse that would be able to get to the top of the cylinder.'
'A clockwork mouse with suction pads on its feet.'
'No noise was heard.'
'A silent clockwork mouse with suction pads on its feet.'

49

Named-ideas and action

In understanding one puts together bundle-ideas as a step towards finding named-ideas. One only acts upon named-ideas. This is because named-ideas are known situations and so the right response is also known. Bundle-ideas are temporary collections of ideas to which there is no definite response. A man walks into a room and is seen to be holding 'something which is shiny, quite long and held horizontally'. That is a bundle-idea to which there is no immediate reaction. But if the bundle-idea is changed to the named-idea 'a gun' then you duck for cover at once.

One searches for named-ideas because they indicate the action to be taken and also because they are real available things. A bundle-idea might read: 'a weight which slowly shifts from one container to another.' But you cannot go out and buy such a thing. If, however, you reach the named-idea an 'egg-timer' then you can actually get hold of one.

Trapped

Named-ideas are fixed and permanent collections of ideas. As suggested above, the aim is to find named-ideas as quickly as possible. But there is the risk of being trapped within the fixed rigidity of a named-idea. If from the bundle-idea a 'weight shifting from one side of the cylinder to another slowly' you move automatically to the named-idea an 'egg-timer' there is a risk that you may be trapped and unable to go on to consider such things as water flowing from one container to another or a weight moved by an electric motor. In the same way if you look at the behaviour of any government and quickly apply the named-idea 'Fascist' then you are likely to get trapped by this idea just as any employer who labels every strike 'Communist'.

Stock

It is only possible to use the named-ideas that one has in one's idea store. If there are few ideas then all manner of situations will be finally interpreted in terms of these few ideas. At some stage in understanding one has to end up with named-ideas. So the fewer there are available the more limited will be the understanding of a situation that does not exactly fit any of the available ideas. In the black cylinder experiment a person who could only think in terms of clocks as time-devices would be unable to use any of the explanations which involved such slow processes as ice melting or water dripping from one container to another. Similarly a person who could only think in terms of two work attitudes, 'lazy' and 'dynamic', would be unable to see that someone might appear to be lazy if uninterested in a job but could be dynamic if interested. To do this one would need the third idea 'unmotivated'.

The types of ideas built up into idea stocks could be considered under three headings:

1. *Precise named-ideas.* These include definite objects (dog, horse, bomb), definite labels (democracy, employer, progressive, reactionary, totalitarian), definite behaviour (love, justice, invention), etc.

2. *Vague named-ideas* (porridge words). These include such words as: mechanism, device, arrangement, apparatus, requiron, something, somehow, etc.

3. *Interaction named-ideas.* These ideas refer to processes, to relationships, to interactions. Such ideas are used to bring together other ideas and show how they are related to each other. These are the function words. Examples of interaction ideas are: oppose, combine, modify, enlarge, cause, develop into, etc.

The vague ideas and the interaction ideas are the ones used to make up bundle-ideas. The more ideas one has in these categories the more is one able to construct bundle-ideas which fit a situation accurately. Just as an artist uses different

51

paint-brushes and colours to capture a scene, so the greater
the availability of such ideas the more is one able to understand situations. Nevertheless at the end one is forced to move
from bundle-ideas to named-ideas. And unless one can develop new named-ideas to cover the new bundle-ideas then
one is forced to use the old stock ideas no matter how sensi-
tively a new bundle-idea may have been built up.

Third and fourth level of understanding

Bundle-ideas tend to correspond to the fourth level (L–4)
which describes the 'way it works'. This description is made
up of several ideas and the way they interact. In fact the whole
description could be said to form a bundle-idea. Named-ideas
on the other hand correspond to the third level which is the
process of 'giving it a name'. Here one identifies the process as
being the same as some definite known process, one uses such
named-ideas as electricity, magic, magnets, etc. As seen in
the previous chapter an explanation of the fall of the black
cylinder often consisted solely of a named-idea like electricity
or gravity.

Precise principles and vague general ideas

Precise principles and vague general ideas are at completely
opposite ends of the range of understanding. So it is rather
surprising that it may be impossible to distinguish one from
the other.

A vague general idea belongs to the second level of understanding (porridge words), e.g. 'a mechanism to make the
cylinder over-balance'. A precise principle is put forward
when one has worked through several possible explanations at
the most detailed fifth level and from them all has *extracted*
a basic principle. Thus a precise principle might be used by

someone who could think of *all* the following possible explanations: a lump of ice under one end of the base of the cylinder; air escaping from a chamber through a small hole; an edge made of wax which melted slowly; an edge pulled up by an electric motor; a pin which protrudes through the base. The principle used to cover all these possibilities might be: 'The base of the cylinder changes and so causes the cylinder to fall over.' It would be because he *could* think of all these mechanisms that the precise-principle man chose to state his explanation in this way. Yet from the statement itself one might suppose it was because he *could not* think of any specific mechanism that he used such general terms as 'change in base'.

Ignorance or knowledge

Does the person who puts down 'timing-device' do so because he cannot think of a specific named-idea? Or does he do so because he can think of so many (egg-timer, clock, water moving through fine tube) that he wants to include them all without being trapped by choice of any particular one? From the statement itself there is no way of knowing. So there is the extraordinary position that a vague general idea may be indistinguishable from a precise principle. This means that a level-two statement may be indistinguishable from what is really a level-five statement. Thus as far as other people are concerned a precise-principle statement may be no more useful than a vague general idea. Conversely a vague general idea would seem to be as useful as a precise principle. The real difference is that the precise-principle man knows his explanation is right and could give details if required whereas the vague-idea man does not have any specific explanation. But if the vague idea is general enough (e.g. a mechanism to make the cylinder fall over) then it is very likely to include the right explanation.

It is no wonder that throughout history people have been

completely unable to distinguish general statements (born of ignorance) from precise principles (born of knowledge). Politicians and other leaders might have had a hard time if such distinction were possible. For instance when a leader urged his people to war they were in no position to tell whether this was a precise strategy reached after careful consideration of many alternatives or a vague general idea arising from an inability to think of any more specific strategy. Similarly it is difficult to tell whether a political manifesto asking for an incomes policy is based on a thorough understanding of the employment situation or an ignorance of it.

In scientific analysis there is much data and little action whereas in everyday thinking there is much action but little data.

Scientific inquiry can choose to focus on a tiny field of interest but everyday thinking has to cope with a variety of situations which are not chosen but thrust at it.

As soon as it allows one to do something about a situation then an explanation is detailed enough.

If you have to choose a suitable action it is better to match it to a general explanation which is unlikely to be wrong than a detailed explanation which might well be wrong.

The 'requiron' is a temporary named word to cover the bundle of requirements.

One only acts upon named-ideas.

5

The Basic Thinking Processes

The whole business of thinking appears to involve terribly complicated processes. But even the most complicated processes may be based on very simple steps. For instance computers handle the complicated mathematics that enable man to get to the moon and walk on its surface. Yet the whole complexity of a computer is based on a switch which is so simple that it is only capable of saying yes or no. The palace at Versailles was built by putting one stone on top of another. The immense complexity of the human organism is based on some rather simple chemical reactions. In the same way the complicated business of thinking can be seen to arise from two simple basic processes: 'carry-on' and 'connect-up'. These two simple processes arise directly from the behaviour of the brain. The brain can be looked at as a nerve network impregnated with memory which directs the flickering patterns of activity that flow across the surface. The behaviour of this type of system is described in *The Mechanism of Mind*.* The system is a surprisingly simple one but like a computer is capable of behaviour which is complicated and sophisticated.

Carry-on

'Carry-on' simply means keep going. If you are walking
* Jonathan Cape, 1969; Penguin, 1971

down a street 'carry-on' simply means keep going down that same street. If you are reciting the alphabet and have got as far as A, B, C, D, E, F then carry-on means keep going with G, H, I, etc. If you are half-way through the nursery rhyme 'Jack and Jill went up the hill . . .' then carry-on means keep going to the end. If you are describing someone you might start by talking about his red hair and blue eyes and then carry-on to mention his long nose and cauliflower ears. Carry-on means that having started on something you go on to the end.

But there has to be a something to carry-on with. There has to be a street or an alphabet or a nursery rhyme or a person you know. In thinking this 'something' is a memory pattern. Once you start on this pattern then you carry-on to the end. The memory pattern is really a sequence of ideas which follow one another. Thus in the black cylinder experiment someone might carry-on from the idea of an egg-timer to the idea of a clock. Or from the idea of a mouse to the idea of a mouse running up some steps to reach some food.

Carry-on is a very simple process that happens in any memory system and it is certainly not confined to human thinking. It simply means that one idea follows another.

Connect-up

Carry-on involves moving from one idea to whatever idea follows next. 'Connect-up' means you start with two separate ideas and try and find a way of connecting them up. Connect-up could also be called: 'link-up', 'fill-in', 'close the gap', etc. For instance, a broken goldfish-bowl and paw-marks on the carpet might be connected up by the idea of 'cat'. You are driving along and the car starts to veer to the right. You connect up the normal behaviour of the car to this new behaviour by the idea of a 'puncture'.

Often the connecting up is so smooth that one is not even aware of there having been any gap to begin with. Humour provides a very clear illustration of the connect-up process. It is only when you have connected things up that you see the joke.

The Irishman was wearing one red sock and one green sock.
'That is a most unusual pair of socks you are wearing,' said the Englishman.
'Not really – I've got another pair exactly like it at home.'

How do you break a Newfie's (a Newfoundlander's) fingers?
Answer: By punching him in the nose.

In the first story it is very easy to make the connection. Once one has made the connection then the story as a whole connects up with the traditional view of the wit and eccentricity of the Irish. There is thus a double process of connecting up.

In the second story it is much more difficult to see the joke. This is because one cannot easily see the connection between a punch in the nose and broken fingers. Nor is one aware of the traditional attitude to Newfoundlanders to be found among some other Canadians. The idea is that Newfies always have their fingers in their noses. The joke does not work because the first gap is rather too large and the second gap is not there unless you happen to be Canadian.

Movement

As suggested before, thinking is simply a matter of moving from one idea to another. In the carry-on process this movement happens naturally as one follows along from one idea to another. Movement happens because the ideas have already been set up in a sort of chain by past experience. You know that the footsteps in the corridor belong to the boss because you have learned this by experience – so you carry-on from the sound of the footsteps to the idea of the boss coming in to see what you are up to. So in the carry-on process the movement is natural and in a sense one is a slave to one's past experience.

In the connect-up process, however, one can deliberately generate movement by setting up two ideas and then trying to connect them up. Usually it is a matter not of setting up two ideas but of setting up one idea which is to be connected-up to the present state of affairs. For instance I am already in Cambridge and I set up the idea of 'London', then the connection is: 'How do I get there? – By train.'

A very simple way of showing this connect-up process is to take a word at random from a dictionary and then try and connect it up to whatever problem one is looking at (this procedure is described in detail in my book *Lateral Thinking: a textbook of creativity**). At first sight it may seem unlikely that a random word will connect up with a specific problem. But in fact it often proves so very easy that when this is done at a lecture the audience believes the word and the problem have been deliberately selected beforehand.

Problem: to solve traffic congestion in cities.
Random word: soap.
Connect-up:

1. Soap is slippery . . . lubricate traffic flow through street . . . remove street parking, bus-stops, traffic-lights . . . make it possible to drive very easily in town but not to do much else . . . stopping of any sort only allowed in special stopping areas.

2. Soap is used to remove dirt . . . remove 'dirty' traffic areas (that is, traffic-intensive areas) from residential or shopping areas.

3. Soap is gradually worn away the more it is used . . . have a system whereby heavily used streets get worn away . . . and

* Ward, Lock, 1970.

58

either get wider and easier to use ... or more bumpy and more difficult to drive on ... devise a self-adjusting system whereby use increases use or slows down more use.

Problems and questions

The trouble with the carry-on process is that the movement does not get you where you want to go. You are passively 'carried along' the patterns set up by experience. But with the connect-up process you can get where you want to go. If you know where you want to go you set this up as a 'destination' and then connect up your starting point to this destination. It is like looking at a road map and finding the route from where you are to your destination.

In problem-solving the statement of the problem is no more than the description of your intended destination. 'No traffic congestion in cities', 'a mechanism to make the black cylinder fall over', 'trousers with ink stain removed', are all destinations. The problems would be stated as: 'to solve traffic congestion problems in cities', 'to explain how the black cylinder fell over', 'to remove an ink stain from a pair of trousers'.

Obviously all these problems can be stated as questions: 'How do I remove this ink stain from the trousers?', 'Why does the black cylinder fall over?' What a question really asks is: 'How do I get to this statement?' or 'Show me the way I can get to this statement.' These are but ways of saying: 'Connect up what I already know with what I want to know.'

Jump ahead

This trick of pushing ahead with a question and then connecting up makes a huge difference to thinking because it gives direction. By asking questions you can move where you want to instead of just carrying on along patterns set up by experience. In order to use this process, however, one has to be able to set up the far end of the gap. Setting up the far end of the gap is asking the question. It is also deciding the destination one wants to get to.

Known and unknown destinations

If you know where you want to go it is easy enough to get there. The fascinating thing is that the destination (the question, the far end of the gap) is actually set up by a process of carry-on. For instance: 'I need a new suit and my suits are made by a tailor in London – how do I get to London from here?' or: 'I am asked to explain how the black cylinder fell over – how did the black cylinder fall over?'

The difficulty arises if you do not really know where you are going. 'How do I get to London?' is very different from 'How do I get to somewhere sunny?' How can you establish the far end of the gap unless you can specify the far end of the gap? The answer is the porridge words which we have come across before.

Porridge words

These very useful meaningless words allow one to set up a question in a vague way. This means that one can still ask questions even if one does not have a definite destination. In the example given above 'How do I get to *somewhere* sunny?' the porridge word 'somewhere' allows one to ask a question which is much less specific than 'How do I get to *Majorca*?' In the same way one can ask, 'What is the mechanism that makes the black cylinder fall over?' Some useful porridge words are listed here:

mechanism
device
thing

arrangement
apparatus
something
object
somewhere
requiron (see page 49)

The statement: 'The requiron zooms through the air and has five legs,' is the same as saying, *'The thing we are looking for* zooms through the air and has five legs.' The word requiron can also be used as an explanation: 'He left suddenly because the requiron must have appeared,' which is the same as saying, 'He left suddenly because *the thing for which we are looking* must have appeared.'

The porridge word 'mechanism' can also be used in these different ways:

'What is the mechanism that makes the cylinder fall over?' (Question)
'The cylinder fell over because of a mechanism within it.' (Explanation, L–2)
'You flick the switch which sets off a time-delay mechanism that eventually knocks the cylinder over.' (Black box use)

Porridge words like black boxes are ignorance tools. Just as black boxes allow us to use a mechanism without really knowing how it works so porridge words allow us to make definite statements or ask definite questions when we do not really know what we are talking about. These vague, blurred porridge words have an extremely important part to play in thinking.

Man is stupider than animals

Man may be smarter than animals only because he is stupider. The paradox is that man may be able to go much further in his thinking than animals only because his basic thinking process is less precise.

The short-sighted hen

It would seem obvious that a sharp-sighted hen would be much better off than a short-sighted hen, for good vision is better than poor vision. But this may not always be so. Some grain is placed behind a wire-grating and a hen is placed in front of the grating. The sharp-sighted hen sees the grain at once and goes directly towards it. She is stopped by the grating but so clear and beckoning is the sight of the grain that she spends all her time trying to get through the grating.

On another occasion a short-sighted hen is placed in front of the wire-grating. This hen is so short-sighted that she cannot even see the grain and so wanders about a bit until eventually she stumbles on the grain which she gobbles up. In this story the perfect vision of the sharp-sighted hen immediately *commits her* to an obvious line of action. The blurred vision of the short-sighted hen prevents this immediate commitment and allows things to work out gradually.

The dog with a cold

The shed is full of pots and pans. A dog with an acute sense of smell is let into the shed. At once he sniffs out a plate of meat and makes directly for it without messing around.

On another occasion a dog with a cold in the nose is let into the shed. He cannot smell very well and so spends a long time messing around, nosing here and there and knocking the covers off pans as he tries to locate the meat which he can only smell *vaguely*. Eventually he finds the meat.

The clear-nosed dog is locked in the shed on a different occasion and this time he is not hungry but wants to get out. He spends quite a lot of time hunting around for an escape hole. The dog with the cold, however, finds the hole at once since in

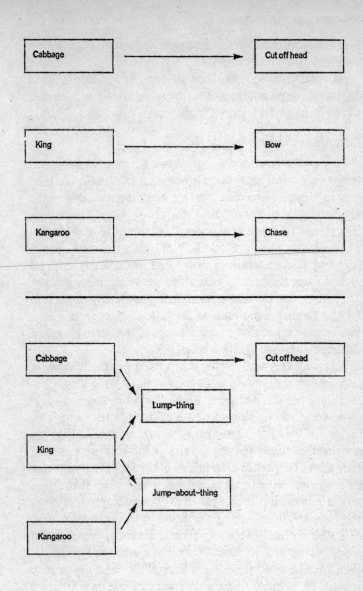

his messing around on the first visit he had come across the hole and noted its position.

As with the short-sighted hen the dog who was able to make an immediate commitment because of his acute senses turned out to be at a disadvantage in the end.

Cabbages and kings

Very acute senses and a sharp brain which can distinguish things very clearly may seem an obvious advantage but they may turn out to be a disadvantage like the good sight of the first hen and the clear nose of the first dog. Good discrimination means that one recognizes things quickly and clearly. There is no messing around. You recognize the special situation at once (grain or meat) and immediately respond with the proper reaction. Action follows recognition directly. The more exact the recognition the more quickly can action follow. Cabbages are seen to be quite distinct from kings. You react to cabbages in a special way. You react to kings in a different way. (See diagram on page 63.)

This is all very well for the sharp brain but the brain with rather poor discrimination finds everything a big blur. Cabbages are not distinct from kings. Both are large 'blurry' objects and so one reacts to both of them in the same way. Instead of being distinguished both cabbages and kings are put together under the vague term 'lump-things'. Later on after a lot of experience the blurry brain does eventually distinguish between cabbages and kings and gives them their proper names. But the vague term 'lump-things' still exists and includes them both – in addition to their proper names.

In a blurry brain large, vague classifications come first and are only later broken down into more specific things. Moreover, because discrimination is so poor the same object may actually be included under a different heading on a different occasion. For instance cabbages and kings may both be regarded as lump-things on one occasion. On another occasion the king may be put together with a kangaroo as a 'jump-about-thing' without any realization that the king is the same king on both occasions. Later even the blurry brain comes to recognize that kangaroos have tails, kings have crowns, and cabbages are green, so they all get sorted out. But the vague general classifications (lump-thing, jump-about-thing) remain.

Cross-links

The vague general classification (lump-things and jump-about-things) are of course the now familiar porridge words. These vague general classifications have the immensely useful function that by providing cross-links they allow the mind to move from one idea to another. The sharp brain at once distinguishes cabbages from kings and no connection between the two is ever formed. A precise response is established for the king situation and a different precise response is established for the cabbage situation. There is no way of getting from one to the other. Nor is there any way of escaping from the precise response that has been established: bow to a king, cut off the head of a cabbage. But with the blurry brain there is this cross-link in so far as cabbages and kings were originally (before one knew better) both regarded as lump-things. So one can get from one idea to another by means of this cross-link.

The sharp brain establishes a series of parallel channels as each specific situation calls forth a specific reaction. But the blurry brain has all sorts of cross-connections which are formed by the vague porridge words. This means that the sharp brain can only react in a fixed manner but the blurry brain can do a lot of 'thinking' as it switches from one idea to another (e.g. since cabbages and kings are both lump-things why not cut off the head of a king?).

Proper philosophers always praise the marvellous ability of the human brain to make abstractions. This means that the brain is able to pick out a feature common to a number of different objects. This common feature is given a nice name and becomes an abstract idea (e.g. lumpiness, jumpiness). This abstracting performance makes the brain sound very marvellous. But sometimes it seems to happen exactly the opposite way round. Instead of the brain being sharp enough to make abstractions it is so blurry that it can only start off with porridge ideas. Later on these get broken down into specific things. So instead of abstractions being marvellously abstracted it may be that the abstractions come first as porridge words which are only later broken down.

As soon as a baby learns to say 'Da-da' it is obvious that every moving object is a Da-da. Later this narrows to every human being. In the next stage Da-da is restricted to men only. Finally Da-da indicates the one true Da-da. This blurry process takes a long time. Yet animals learn to recognize their parents in an infallible way within an hour of being born. This recognition is not instinct but learning, as shown by Konrad Lorenze, who got down on hands and knees and quacked a bit and instantly and permanently became the mother for some newly hatched mallard ducklings.

It is because the human brain is such a blurry thing that babies take so long to grow up and get going. Baby animals (e.g. deer, horses and especially other herd animals) almost 'hit the deck running'. They are already equipped with certain inbuilt instinct responses which do not have to be learned.

They have very sharp senses and sharp brains which enable them to distinguish things clearly and so learn very quickly. Quick learning depends on good discrimination. It is only blurring and confusion which slows down learning.

Thus one ends up with the curious situation that man is able to think better than animals because his brain is blurry whereas theirs are clear and sharp.

Tortoises win races

The advantage of having a sharp brain is that you can react quickly. Without the unnatural wire-fence the sharp-sighted hen would have got to the grain and gobbled it up before the short-sighted one got going. Similarly the clear-nosed dog would have eaten up the meat before the dog with a cold could get to it. So in a competitive world the sharp-brained animals who can act quickly are more likely to survive than the blurry-brained creatures. Similarly the animals which are born ready for action are more likely to survive than those who have to stumble around helpless for years before they can even feed themselves.

But if – somehow – the blurry-brained animals can survive, then they will eventually end up far ahead. The sharp-brained animals establish a few quick and efficient reaction patterns and then become trapped by these. The blurry-brained animals mess around with porridge ideas which allow them to move from idea to idea in what we call thinking.

Summary of porridge words

Porridge words have been mentioned in different places in the preceding chapters. It is convenient to sum up their usefulness at this point.

Porridge words are rather meaningless words. It is precisely because they are meaningless that they are so immensely useful in thinking. They act as link words to keep thought moving from one idea to another. If there were no such words then thinking would come to a dead end when there was no direct step to another specific idea. The various uses are listed below:

1. Porridge words allow one to set up vague questions when one has not enough information to ask a specific question.

2. Porridge words offer usable explanations when one cannot provide any more detail.

3. Porridge words act as cross-links for movement from one idea to another.

4. Porridge words can act as black boxes to enable one to leap-frog over an area of ignorance and carry on.

5. Porridge words prevent too early a commitment to a specific idea and so keep options open as long as possible.

The paradox is that porridge words arise from ignorance and yet they become immensely useful thinking tools in their own right.

The curious thing is that over the centuries intellectual tradition in the West (but not in the East) has been directed against porridge words and in favour of precise ideas. The sharp-brained intellectuals have set up ideas which have as much fixity and rigidity as the responses of sharp-brained animals. It is not often realized that it is the blurry-brained creative people who have established new general ideas and then gone on to make them more specific. The sharp-brained outlook can never establish new ideas because it does not mess around, never makes mistakes, and is completely trapped by existing ideas. It is curious that we so encourage the sharp-brained attitude when the advantage of the human brain depends on the blurry quality which makes for creativity. Sharp brains are indeed essential but only for refining, developing and using the ideas thrown up by blurry-brained thinking. And computers are of course very sharp-brained creatures which can do this work for us.

Just as black boxes allow us to use a mechanism without really knowing how it works so porridge words allow us to make definite statements or ask definite questions when we do not really know what we are talking about.

The sharp-brained animals establish a few quick and efficient reaction patterns and then become trapped by these.

It is not often realized that it is the blurry-brained creative people who have established new general ideas and then gone on to make them more specific.

The sharp-brained outlook can never establish new ideas because it does not mess around, never makes mistakes, and is completely trapped by existing ideas.

6

The Five Ways to be Wrong

Some characteristic mistakes are a natural part of the thinking process. These mistakes cannot be avoided because they arise directly from the way the mind works. One can no more have successful thinking without these mistakes than one can have a petrol engine without exhaust gases. Five out of the most fundamental mistakes are outlined here. These mistakes occur so often that in the black cylinder experiment just one type of mistake occurred in 34 per cent of the specific explanations offered. This is a surprisingly high percentage when one considers that those taking part in the experiment were all highly educated.

M–1 The monorail mistake

'The kitten has been out in the rain and is soaking wet. I'll pop her in the spin-dryer for a few minutes because that is how Mummy dries wet things.' The much dizzied kitten did actually survive this monorail mistake.

'These pills are red and must be sweets,' says the child helping himself to a handful of iron tablets from the bathroom cabinet.

'Wild rabbits provide good shooting so let's import some from England,' reasoned Thomas Austin in Australia in 1859 and he imported twenty-four which then multiplied to the extent that they have caused millions of pounds' worth of damage.

The monorail mistake occurs when you follow along a single track directly from one idea to another:

wet – spin-dryer
red – sweets
sport – rabbits

Lean against it

If you were to lean something against a free-standing cylinder you could knock it over. So one moves directly from the idea of leaning something against the black cylinder to its falling over. Since nothing was seen to be leaning against the cylinder on the outside one moves on to the idea that something must have been leaning against the wall on the inside.

In one black cylinder explanation a heavy rod balanced on its point falls slowly through treacle to lean against the cylinder side and knock it over. (See picture on page 72.)

In another a number of rods fall one by one against the cylinder side until there is enough weight to make it fall over. (See picture on page 72.)

There were several other explanations like these. None of them could work. By going directly in monorail fashion from the idea of a weight leaning against the cylinder on the outside to a weight leaning against the cylinder wall on the inside one ignores the fact that a weight on the outside is independent of the cylinder but a weight resting on the cylinder floor pins this to the ground and so prevents the cylinder falling over. A very beautiful example of this particular monorail mistake is shown in the sequence of pictures on page 73. An object shaped as in (A) would fall over. So if the object were placed against the side of the cylinder (B) it would knock the cylinder over. This would also happen if the object was placed inside the cylinder (C). But if the cylinder fell over after a period of time the top-heavy object would have to form slowly. Now an even layer of sand placed across the top of the cylinder

71

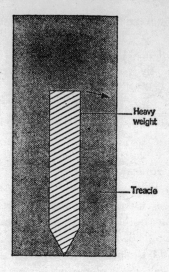

Heavy weight

Treacle

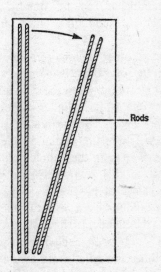

Rods

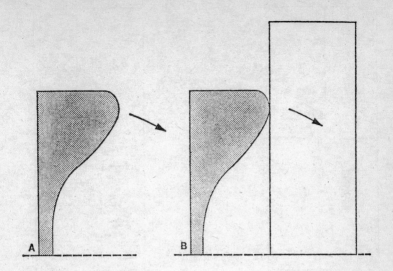

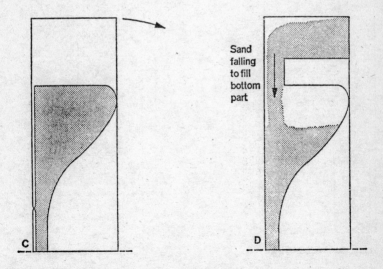

Sand
falling
to fill
bottom
part

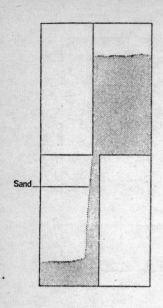

Sand

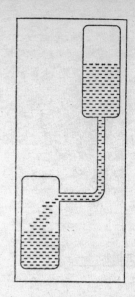

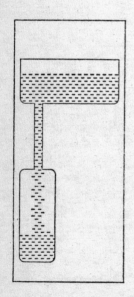

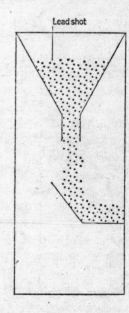

Lead shot

would be symmetrical and would not upset it (D). But if this sand trickled down to slowly fill the original shape then there would come a time when the cylinder would be knocked over. This is a beautiful example of a double monorail mistake because the explanation moves straight on from a top-heavy object leaning against the outside of the cylinder to its leaning against the inside and then on to the gradual formation of this top-heavy object. Even if this top-heavy object could knock the cylinder over it would do so at once for the sand spread in the upper compartment would still make it top-heavy without having to trickle through to the bottom.

Weight to one side

This is another example of the monorail mistake as it occurred in the black cylinder explanations. If people sit evenly in a small boat it is stable but if they all move to one side it capsizes. If you place things evenly on the breakfast tray it is stable but if you put everything at one end it is inclined to tip up. If you have a stack of books and you add some more books but place them to one side the stack may tumble down.

5·6 per cent of the black cylinder explanations suggested directly that the cylinder fell over 'because there was a shift of weight to one side'. So strong is the idea that a 'shift of weight' will make the cylinder overbalance that some explanations (as in picture on the opposite page) simply show a weight moving from one side to the other. Another idea on the opposite page shows how fluid flows from a half-full tank on one side to fill a half-full tank on the other so giving a full tank on one side and an empty tank on the other. Another lot of explanations start with an evenly distributed weight which then shifts to one side (as shown in pictures on the opposite page). Water, sand and lead shot were used to provide these slowly shifting weights.

All these explanations suffer from the monorail mistake. Weight which is not placed evenly or which shifts to one side does cause some things to overbalance so one moves directly

to the idea of a shifting weight to make the cylinder fall over.
But what is *ignored* is the fact that a shift in weight only causes
instability when the centre of gravity comes to fall outside the
base (overhang, as in a stack of books) or when the object is
only balanced in the beginning by the even distribution of
weight (as in a boat or a see-saw) and this would imply that
the cylinder had a rounded bottom.

Top-heavy

This is another monorail-type mistake. Everyone knows
that top-heavy things overbalance and fall over. In fact the
very word 'top-heavy' means that a thing cannot be stood
upright. So in monorail fashion one goes directly from 'top-
heavy' to 'falling over'. All one has to do is to make the
cylinder top-heavy and it will fall over.

'Cylinder fell due to becoming top-heavy.'
'Something at the bottom rose to make it top-heavy so it
overbalanced.'
'Became top-heavy by redistribution of internal mass.'
'A weight inside the tube which moved slowly up the tube
and therefore made the tube top-heavy.'
'Something was moving up inside the tube so it eventually
overbalanced.'
'Some fluid inside evaporating and so going into the second
chamber at the top – solidifying and making the cylinder top-
heavy.'
(Of course if a thing is getting top-heavy it must be getting
comparatively lighter at the bottom.)
'Cylinder fell down because it got progressively lighter at
the base.'

13 per cent of the specific explanations gave top-heaviness
as the reason for the cylinder falling over.
Various devices were used for moving a weight to the top of
the cylinder: mouse running up steps for food; electric
motor and hoist; fluid evaporating in a bottom chamber and

condensing in a higher one; boiling fluid as in a coffee machine; insects clustering around a light at the top, etc. One way of moving the weight to the top of the cylinder provides a most interesting example of the monorail mistake. (See picture below.)

A weight with a specific gravity slightly lower than that of the fluid in the cylinder floats upwards to the top of the cylinder so making it top-heavy. The monorail sequence is clear: to make cylinder top-heavy get a weight to the top – to get weight to top slowly make it float upwards. In fact something only floats upwards if it is *lighter* than the fluid in which it is immersed (e.g. a cork or a bubble of air are lighter than water); if it is heavier it sinks. So anything that floated upwards would actually be lighter than the surrounding fluid so instead of moving a 'weight' to the top one would actually be moving a 'lightness' and the cylinder would become *less* top-heavy. The monorail mistake seems incredible but it follows very easily because one moves directly from the idea of a

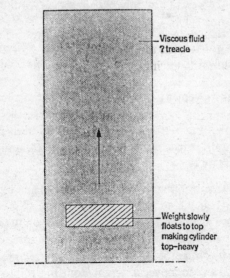

Viscous fluid ? treacle

Weight slowly floats to top making cylinder top-heavy

weight moving to the top to the idea of a weight floating and ignores the fact that if it did this it would cease to be a 'weight'.

Top-heaviness as a cause for the fall of the cylinder is itself a monorail mistake. Top-heavy things do fall over and are impossible to stand upright but this is not simply because they are top-heavy. In addition to the high centre of gravity there has to be a slant so that the centre of gravity falls outside the base or alternatively a rounded base so that the cylinder would start to slant over until the centre of gravity did fall outside the base. If there was such a slant then a rising weight would overbalance the cylinder eventually.

It is a monorail mistake to go directly from the idea of top-heaviness to instability and ignore the necessary circumstances of a slant or a rounded base.

Top-heavy and to one side

This monorail mistake combines both the two previous ones. Here the weight not only rises to the top of the cylinder but also to one side.

'Weight which was not concentric with the circular base travelling upwards up the tube until centre of gravity causes tube to fall.'

'Gradual movement of weight up one side from base to top.'

'An electric engine (battery operated) has been pulling a weight up until it reaches the top – off centre – and this unbalances the tube.'

Various ways of moving a weight to the top and to one side were suggested, including: a tiny man who climbed up a ladder placed against one wall of the cylinder on the inside; a mouse climbing up pins set in the wall to reach some cheese at the top; an electric motor which rotated a vertical rod with a spiral thread and so moved a weight along this rod to the top; a heating coil which boiled liquid in a bottom compartment and so forced it into an upper compartment as in a coffee percolator.

Shift in centre of gravity

A large number of explanations (15 per cent) simply indicated a 'shift in the centre of gravity'. It was assumed that if the cylinder was stable then a shift in the centre of gravity would make it fall over. The monorail mistake is obvious: shift in centre of gravity – overbalance. This ignores the other circumstances which have to be present before a shift in the centre of gravity will make something fall over (i.e. overhang, slope, rounded bottom, etc., or anything which will make the centre of gravity fall outside the base).

'Delayed-action spring-loaded mechanism which changes centre of gravity.'

'Shift of centre of gravity.'

'Mechanism involving change of centre of gravity through change of temperature by atmospheric action.'

'Centre of gravity shifted.'

'It contains sand which changes centre of gravity as it runs down.'

Monorail mistake is easy to make

The monorail mistake is extremely easy to make because thinking involves moving on from one idea to the next one. In this simple movement one tends to ignore the other factors which are part of the original situation. If two things come together to give an effect then it is easy to take only one of these things and to expect the effect. For instance a child watching his mother fry chips might try his hand by putting chips into a pan over the stove without thinking that oil was required. In exactly the same way the shifts in weight suggested as black cylinder explanations were inadequate by themselves.

In a way monorail mistakes are simple-minded mistakes. 'Taxes are unfair – let's abolish taxes.' 'We want more money – let's strike for more money.' 'Teachers are there to teach – so teachers know more about teaching than anyone else.' 'Professors are clever – so what he says must be right.' The monorail mistake simply involves going directly from one idea to another in an inevitable manner and ignoring all qualifying factors. Of course if one cannot think of any qualifying factors then one has no choice but to ignore them. So it can be quite difficult to convince someone making a monorail mistake that there are other things to be taken into account for you cannot deny the validity of the move from one idea to another. 'But top-heavy things do fall over – can you deny that?'

M–2 The magnitude mistake

This is the second major mistake which arises directly from the way the mind works. Here the mind moves from one idea to another in what seems to be a valid way if one looks only at the *name* of the ideas but is not valid if one looks at the magnitudes involved.

'Mummy, you need not buy anything for dinner because Daddy has just caught a fish.'
'We'll clear up crime in the streets by putting more policemen on the beat.'

The movement from the idea of the fish to the idea of eating it for dinner is perfectly valid but the magnitude may be all wrong if the fish caught by Daddy happens to be a two-inch tiddler. In the same way it is obvious that more policemen would stop crime but three extra policemen would not make enough difference and it might be necessary to more than double the police force.

In the black cylinder experiment the magnitude mistake was often made.

'The black cylinder fell over when everyone picked up their pens to write at the same time – breeze blew it over.'

'Draught from door – sure it's a basic reason.'

'Vibration from fan and overhead projector knocked it over.'

'Heavy tread shook floor and so knocked cylinder over.'

'Lecturer's backward tread on platform shook table.'

'Sound of laughter from audience unbalanced it.'

'You knocked it over when no one was looking.'

Other examples include the accumulation of insects around a light at the top of the cylinder to make it top-heavy and magnetic effects acting over distances up to a foot to pull the cylinder over.

All these explanations *could* work if the magnitude was right but would certainly *not* work if the magnitude was wrong. A very strong breeze could knock over a very light cylinder or one that was very finely balanced. But in fact there was no perceptible breeze and the cylinder was heavy enough to make a loud thump (noted by several of the audience) when it fell over. Furthermore the cylinder was put down casually without the care needed to put down something that was finely balanced. Also it would be very unlikely that a breeze of any strength would be generated even if everyone did pick up their pens at the same time.

The floor happened to be solid concrete and the lecturers' platform was also of heavy construction so vibration caused by a tread would be slight. The fan and overhead projector were about fifteen feet away and on a separate table so their slight vibration was unlikely to knock the cylinder over. It is highly unlikely that the lecturer could *guarantee* a moment when none of the audience were looking in order to walk across and knock the cylinder over. A collection of small insects would not provide much weight. It would require a very powerful magnet to act over a distance of one foot and something more than a torch battery to power it.

In all these cases the *name* of the effect is right but the *size* is wrong. Magnets do attract things without being in contact but they have to be quite close. Children's thinking is full of magnitude mistakes. One design for building a house quickly had a man standing on the roof of a building holding a magnet which attracted magnetic bricks from a truck below. A design for an apple-picking machine had a magnet buried in the ground at the foot of the apple tree. A metal tag was attached to each apple and when the magnet was switched on the apples were pulled to the ground.

A man sets out to walk from London to Liverpool in an evening. You tell him it is impossible but he points to the signpost and says, 'This is the right road, isn't it?' You cannot deny that it is the right road – only point out that the distance is too great. Similarly in the magnitude mistake the movement from one idea to another is perfectly valid – but the magnitude may be quite wrong.

Abstract ideas

The magnitude mistake is unlikely to occur in situations of which one has had direct experience. For instance a carpenter will look at a piece of wood and say, 'That will be strong enough to support my weight.' That is why children so often make magnitude mistakes when drawing things of which they have no direct experience – when they are just putting named-ideas together.

Thinking usually involves thinking ahead rather than describing the scene of the moment. So it involves putting together named-ideas in a way which may not have been experienced. Thus the magnitude mistake is very likely to occur. This is especially so when one is dealing with abstract ideas like love, power, justice, unrest, punishment, fear, greed, etc. 'Love conquers all.' But how much love is needed to conquer an outside lavatory, no hot water and a husband who prefers alcohol to work? 'Diet and you will lose weight.' Maybe – but how much dieting and for how long? 'Punishment is the best way of maintaining law and order.' But how much punishment?

Measurement

Measurement is the tool we have deliberately created to cope with the magnitude mistake. 'Put a *teaspoonful* of shampoo into a *cupful* of water,' is quite different from 'Put the shampoo in water.' We have invented the number system which allows us to break up a continuous range of sizes into separate named parts. An eight-pound Christmas turkey is a very different thing from a thirteen-pound turkey. It is as different as a red dress is from a blue dress. By means of numbers and measurement we split up a named-idea into several other named-ideas. A mother does not order a 'turkey' for Christmas and run the risk of an awful magnitude mistake but orders a 'thirteen-pound turkey' – just as one would order coffee if one wanted coffee and tea if one wanted tea and not just a 'drink' in a café.

Without numbers it is perfectly correct to say, 'Daddy has caught a fish – we can all eat it for dinner.' This may be right if Daddy has indeed caught a big enough fish or it could be horribly wrong if Daddy is not so skilful. But if the message had been, 'Daddy has caught a two-ounce tiddler,' then it would be quite clear that whereas one could go from the idea of 'fish' to 'dinner' one could not possibly go from the idea of 'two-ounce fish' to 'dinner'.

Names not measurement

The trouble is that in most cases there are no units of measurement or indeed any way of measuring. What are the units of war, organization, social justice, beauty, impatience, sensitivity, boredom, happiness, etc.? We have only just started

83

to develop ways of measuring such an obvious thing as pain so that we can compare the effectiveness of different pain-killers.

One can of course use adjectives to indicate size. But these are almost useless because they are so relative. 'You cannot put a big fish in that small boat,' means very little. What is meant by big fish? Is it a big fish for these parts or a big fish as fishes go or an absolute big fish like a twenty-foot shark? If all it means is that you cannot put into the boat a fish that is too big to go into the boat then one is not really saying anything at all.

Adjectives refer only to the object they describe and are not independent indications of size: a big fish as fish go in these parts, a small boat as boats go, etc.

A hen can lay an egg but a hen cannot lay an *ostrich* egg. It is easy to deal with magnitude if different *sizes* of thing have completely different *names* because then one simply treats them as different things. For instance one could describe skirts as very long, long, short, very short. Or one could actually talk in terms of inches above the ground or inches above the knee. Or one could simply say mini-skirt, midi-skirt and maxi-skirt. Similarly with wine one could specify the number of pints and ounces in a bottle or one could give different names to the different sizes: bottle, magnum, demi-john, jeroboam, methuselah.

The trouble is that for many things we have never developed separate names based on differences of size. For instance with love, justice, power, we are left with the simple idea. This means that one is always making magnitude mistakes. Perhaps if one had seven words for love like the Greeks it would be easier. Even if one could say mini-love, midi-love and maxi-love it might help to diminish magnitude errors. 'How can you love me if you insist on reading in bed at night?' could be answered by 'I have a maxi-love for you which is not altered by this mini-inconvenience.'

Similarly we have but one word for justice and law. So a

boy who steals an apple, a motorist who parks too long and a murderer are all breaking the *law* and all must be dealt with by *justice*. So the courts get clogged and people's lives get ruined by labels because we have not developed a way of breaking down the large idea of justice into smaller ones to minimize the magnitude mistake. At last we are beginning to do this in the situation of 'war' by setting up a series of graded steps instead of only having war/no war as we used to have. We can now have stages of escalation such as: stage of threats; stage of border incidents; stage of mobilization, etc. This is the equivalent of saying: one warfare unit; two warfare units; three warfare units, etc. The result is that one can match magnitudes instead of saying, 'There is a border incident, this means full-scale war,' as we used to.

M–3 The misfit mistake

You are walking down the street and you recognize the back-view of someone you know very well. The back of his head is unmistakable and the suit is one he often wears. You quicken your pace and draw level – only to find it is a total stranger.

There is a tiny fish which picks the parasites off the fins and scales of much larger fish. The large fish recognize this helpful little fellow and even open their mouths so that the tiny fish can swim inside and scavenge around. But another tiny fish looks like the first fish and has even learned the same little dance. So the big fish thinking the deceitful fish is the usual friend lets it get near – whereupon the fish nibbles large bits out of the fin of the big fish.

In both the above examples something is recognized as being familiar but actually turns out to be something quite different. This is the misfit mistake because the idea of what something is does not *fit* reality. You recognize something by noticing certain features and these features lead you on to a familiar idea such as a person you know or a fish you know. You do not wait until you have listed every possible feature before you jump to a conclusion. You do this as soon as you can. Yet if you had noticed other features you might have changed your mind and so avoided the misfit mistake. For instance if you had noticed that the man in the street ahead of you had rings on his fingers then at once you would have known it could not have been your friend.

In the black cylinder experiment there were several explanations which made the misfit mistake by jumping to a conclusion which did not fit with the actual information available to the viewers.

For instance many of the explanations suggested that the cylinder was so very light that it fell over on its own or was blown over by a slight breeze. This was clearly a misfit mistake since the cylinder was heavy enough to make a loud bang as it fell over. Several explanations suggested that the bottom part of the cylinder was filled with a substance like 'silly putty' which slowly gives way. The cylinder would thus sag and then fall over. But the cylinder was not seen to sag and then fall over – it fell over abruptly.

Another explanation showed a weight which rotated eccentrically about the vertical shaft of an electric motor. This would have made the cylinder wobble about until it fell over. But the cylinder could not be seen to wobble about.

Every single one of the cylinder explanations was wrong in the sense that no explanation described what was actually in the cylinder. Thus in a sense they were all misfit mistakes because they assumed something to be what it was not. But in practice one can only go on the information that is actually available. One can never do better than this. One cannot pretend that one can ever have all possible information – and certainly this was not the case in the black cylinder experiment. So in practice the mistake occurs when an idea does not fit with the information *that is actually available*.

One jumps to a conclusion based on the features one has

noticed. If these are only a fraction of what could have been noticed then a misfit mistake may well be made. If one does base a conclusion on all the available information then that conclusion is as valid as it can be in the circumstances. But if someone else comes along and offers new information then the idea may have to be changed or it becomes a misfit mistake.

Goodness of fit

It is important to realize that the amount of misfit does not indicate the size of the mistake. There would be no difference in the actual mistake whether the man you mistakenly recognized in the street had only one feature in common with your friend or nineteen features out of twenty. In both cases it would simply not have been who you thought it was. The mistake may be more understandable and forgivable if there are a lot of features in common but in practical terms it is just the same mistake. The old Newtonian view of the universe had only a very tiny degree of misfit. Einstein's view fitted just a little better. But the outcome of the two ideas was very different especially when one considers how atomic energy came from Einstein's view.

A theory or idea which has 95 per cent fit is not necessarily more correct than one with only 70 per cent fit. Both may be useful but both need changing.

Easy to make

The misfit mistake is very easy to make because the mind cannot really notice all there is to be noticed. The mind works by using well-established patterns. The speed and effectiveness of its action depend on recognizing these patterns as soon as possible. One does not wait to notice all possible features but jumps quickly from a few features to recognition of the situation. The more familiar the situation the quicker the jump to recognition. Thus if one has very definite and very strong ideas one jumps to conclusions very quickly – and makes a lot of misfit mistakes. Some time ago in New York a policeman walked over to a stalled car. The man in the car fumbled for his driving licence. The policeman thought he was going for a gun and shot at him. Whereupon the other man shot back. The man in the car was in fact an off-duty policeman. A wife who is very suspicious of her husband will quickly interpret such things as a difference in the level of his tie-ends at the end of the day from the beginning as evidence of infidelity, whereas he may just have played squash at midday. A person with strong political views will make misfit mistake after misfit mistake as he jumps to conclusions which do not fit the available facts.

M–4 The must-be mistake

This is the arrogance mistake. Unlike the other mistakes it is a mistake in the future rather than in the present or the past. It is a mistake not in the idea but in the way it is prevented from developing. There may be nothing wrong with the way information has been put together to reach a conclusion. The mistake only arises when arrogance clamps down on this conclusion and fixes it.

Stops evolution

An arrogance-clamp prevents any improvement in an idea. The clamp stops the normal evolutionary process by which ideas can get better and better. To halt evolution at some point is to claim that further evolution cannot improve the idea. It is like supposing that animal evolution ought to have stopped at the dinosaurs because they suited the environment so well. But circumstances change and ideas have to change with them in order to keep pace. It is not so much the inventiveness of twentieth-century technology that causes trouble but the lack of inventiveness in the nineteenth-century ideas that control the technology. We still believe that if you have a plane it is nice to have a bigger and faster plane. We still have nineteenth-century ideas on conflict but twentieth-century weapons.

But even if circumstances do not change, a particular idea can never make the best use of available information because of the way the brain works (see *The Mechanism of Mind*; and de Bono's 1st law in chapter 9). An idea which is a putting together of information that has trickled into the mind over a period of time continues to improve as that information is re-sorted and rearranged. In this process the idea gets closer and closer to the best use of available information. So even if circumstances do not change an arrogance-clamp prevents the improvement of ideas.

Shuts out alternatives

In addition to stopping the evolution of an idea the must-be mistake shuts out the possibility of other ideas. These other ideas are not excluded because they are inadequate but simply because the idea guarded by arrogance seems adequate enough. Even if the other ideas are not at the moment as satisfactory as the one guarded by arrogance if they had some attention they might well develop to the point where they were superior. Furthermore the must-be mistake shuts out the possibility of a completely new point of view which has not yet been generated. Not only is no effort made to generate such an alternative but it would be ignored even if it happened along by chance.

There is nothing wrong in saying that the black cylinder fell over because a pin protruded suddenly from the base. The must-be mistake arises when one declares that this is the *only* possible way it could have happened.

Culture and personality

The must-be mistake does arise from the way the mind handles information but it also arises from the traditional tools that we have developed for thinking. This is especially so with the YES/NO system with its rigid acceptances and rejections. In practice the must-be mistake with its attendant arrogance is also related to personality and training.

M–5 The miss-out mistake

This could also be called the selectivity mistake or the partial choice mistake. It arises when someone considers only part of a situation and yet reaches conclusions that are applied to the whole situation. For instance friends might sympathize with a wife whose husband has run away and roundly condemn the irresponsibility of the man. They would overlook the fact that she had driven him away by her nagging.

In the miss-out mistake the conclusion is always perfectly valid with respect to the starting point. For instance a photograph of a policeman hitting a man with a club may be used as evidence of police brutality which is what it looks like. What may be missed out is the fact that the man has a knife with which he has just attacked the policeman. It may be quite impossible to tell this from the photograph.

The whole picture

It is easy enough to recognize a miss-out mistake when you can see the whole picture. But there is no way of telling what has been missed out unless *you already know* the whole picture. If you do not already know this why should you believe that there is more to the picture than you have been shown? To believe that you are only being shown part of a picture you have to have some special reasons – for instance suspicion of the person who is showing you the picture. Even if you do have this suspicion that there must be a fuller picture somewhere you may have no way of finding it and you are left with the vague impression that it must be there somewhere. You now have several choices:

1. You reject the conclusion that is offered because you are *somehow* convinced that it is based on only part of the picture.

2. You reject the conclusion that has been offered because you do not like it and hence claim that it must be based on only part of the picture.

3. You accept the conclusion with reservations but still look around for the complete picture.

4. You accept the conclusion because you like it and decide the picture is after all complete.

5. Since you cannot find the rest of the picture you conclude that it is not really there and that you do have the whole picture.

Selection

Political or ideological propaganda of any sort is always based on the miss-out mistake. Usually it is so selective that one might even call it the 'pick-out' mistake rather than the 'miss-out' one. You look at that part of the whole picture which will give you the conclusions you want to make. As in advertising you pick out the selling features and ignore the rest. Fortunately selling ideas is not yet as sophisticated as selling washing-powder. You look at the richness of a capitalist to contrast it with the poverty of a worker but you ignore the productivity of the economy. Or you look at the absence of capitalist inequality in a political system but fail to notice the lack of personal freedom. Someone else might look at the productivity of a capitalist system and miss out the poverty or fear of poverty that fuels it. It is easy enough to reach whatever conclusions one wants and then to cut out that part of the picture which leads to these conclusions. The rest is of course missed out.

Attention area

The miss-out mistake is not usually dishonest or deliberate. It is all a matter of where one draws the boundaries of the area of attention. For it is within this area that one is going to think and draw conclusions. Does the number of minutes for which you boil an egg include the consideration that it has been kept in the refrigerator or that you are in a mountain-top resort? Does social justice include the rate of expansion of the economy? Is poverty related to yesterday's conditions, today's comparisons or tomorrow's possibilities? One has to draw boundaries somewhere and they are usually drawn by the extent of one's interest. The miss-out mistake arises not because one draws boundaries but because one applies a conclusion based on a certain part of the picture to the whole picture. For instance one might argue that socialized medicine was a failure because one had to wait two years to have varicose veins operated upon.

Summary

The most important point is that the mistakes arise directly from the way the mind handles information. They are not a matter of individual stupidity or carelessness or lack of training. Even the most intelligent and highly educated people make exactly the same type of mistake. They may be dealing with ideas like political stability rather than the building of a garden shed but the type of mistake is the same. This is hardly surprising since the mistakes arise directly from the way the mind handles information. The same processes that make it so effective a thinking device are also responsible for the mistakes. You cannot have electricity that will give you all the power you want but not give you a shock because a shock is only the same power applied to your body. What you do in practice is to become aware of the shock danger and take steps to minimize or avoid the danger. In the same way you learn to recognize the mistakes of mind and to minimize the danger by developing new thinking tools and attitudes.

Correcting mistakes

The easier mistake to correct is the misfit mistake. If someone points out to you something which you have overlooked then you may at once change your mind of your own accord. For instance in the example of the mistaken recognition of the man walking down the street: if a companion had pointed out that the man wore rings on his fingers you would have changed your mind at once. But if there is no one around to point things out then it is quite likely that you will go on neglecting what you neglected in the first place because your idea seems right enough to you. Thus the views of others are particularly helpful in avoiding misfit mistakes.

Misfit mistakes are not always easy to reverse. If the person really needs the idea he is holding then he is unlikely to change it if you point out areas where it does not fit. Thus someone who regards all foreign immigrants as a drain on the social services is unlikely to change this view if you point out that most contribute more than they receive.

A very difficult mistake to overcome is the monorail mistake. This is because the sequence seems logically correct and we have always placed so much trust in logical correctness that we refuse to budge from something that is logically correct. It is no use pointing out that the direct move from one idea to another is only possible if other things are taken into account. Thus it is no use pointing out that a top-heavy thing only falls over if the base is rounded because that is not the way the idea has been set up in the first place. The best way is to accept the idea but follow it further. Instead of saying, 'You cannot put the wet kitten into the spin-dryer because that is for clothes,' you say, 'If you do put the kitten in the spin-dryer the kitten will die.' By accepting the idea but carrying it further one can often show why it is wrong. For instance one might say, 'Suppose all top-heavy things did fall over. What about a sort of pyramid shape which was very heavy at the top – would it fall over?' The other way is to reduce the arrogance with which logically correct ideas are held but this is to do with the arrogance mistake.

The magnitude mistake falls somewhere between the two above as regards difficulty of correction. There are times when one can actually explore the magnitudes involved and quote sizes and figures. For instance if someone argues that since everyone fears cancer no one will smoke cigarettes if they are declared to produce cancer you can show that the actual fall in cigarette smoking after the announcement was only a small percentage and transitory. If someone argues that people like watching violence on TV you could set out to count how many people did actually prefer to watch violence.

But most of the time one does not have the data or actual magnitudes and then the magnitude mistake is very hard to budge. This is because it becomes a matter of logical sequence. The person points to the signpost and says, 'This is the road to Liverpool – can you deny it?' And of course you cannot. Logically unrest can be said to lead to revolution just as a hen can be said to lead to an egg. But a hen does not lay an ostrich egg and a little natural unrest need not lead to full-scale revolution.

Sometimes one can use the ostrich-egg strategy for overcoming magnitude mistakes. This means giving things different names if they have different sizes, e.g. puddle, pond, lake, for an idea of water. But such named-ideas have to exist already. They cannot be manufactured on the spot. There is also the difficulty that the mind prefers to work at extreme ends of the spectrum when it comes to matters which are not physical in nature. For instance it is much easier to declare that one is madly in love than to use other terms on the love scale such as attracted, interested, compatible, in a state of liking, etc. All these other terms sound weak just as 'unrest' sounds weak when one prefers to talk of 'revolution'.

By far the hardest mistake to overcome is the must-be mistake (arrogance). This is because it is not really a mistake at the moment. There may actually be nothing wrong with the idea that is being held with so much arrogance. One can only see the mistake when one pays attention to what the arrogance shuts out. The mistake arises when one compares the idea as it is to the way it could develop were it not prevented by arrogance from changing at all. But it is extremely difficult to give this potential view to someone who does not have it. With the must-be mistake the fault is not in the idea itself but in the way it is held or imposed on other people.

The miss-out mistake (selectivity) is sometimes difficult to overcome and sometimes easy. It is usually quite easy to show that the point of view adopted by the mistake-maker is a special point of view that only covers part of the situation. What happens next depends on how this special point of view was chosen. If it was chosen deliberately in order to make some point then the person will stick to it and insist that it is the most important point of view even if there *are* other points of view. If, however, the special point of view has been chosen innocently the other person may be prepared to recognize the limitation of that point of view and even perhaps switch to a better one. In the difficult cases the first step is to try and get acceptance of the fact that you are each looking at different parts of the situation. Once you have that acceptance then the miss-out mistake disappears for the mistake only occurs when someone looks at only part of the situation and assumes he is looking at the whole. If someone looks at a part of a situation and accepts that it is only part, then there is no mistake.

Mistakes arise directly from the way the mind handles information not through stupidity or carelessness.

The same processes that make the mind so effective a thinking device are also responsible for the mistakes.

The monorail mistake simply involves going directly from one idea to another in an inevitable manner and ignoring all qualifying factors.

Measurement is the tool we have created deliberately to cope with the magnitude mistake.

The misfit mistake is very easy to make because the mind cannot really notice all there is to be noticed.

The must-be mistake is a mistake in the future rather than in the present or in the past.

The must-be mistake can be recognized when one compares the idea as it is to the way it could develop were it not prevented by arrogance from changing at all.

An arrogance-clamp stops the normal evolutionary process by which ideas can get better and better.

The miss-out mistake arises when a conclusion that is based on only part of the situation is applied to the whole situation.

7

The Four Ways to be Right

The need to be right

The practical purpose of thinking is to enable us to understand what is going on around us so that we can react in a suitable way and also alter things to our advantage. To carry out this purpose effectively thinking must come up with right answers – at least most of the time. In fact the need to be right seems to be very much stronger than the practical requirement that thinking should be effective. This strong need to be right has much to do with the ego and seems to be based on two things:

1. The fear-based need to understand the unknown for the sake of security.
2. The huge emphasis placed by education on the need to be right.

Understanding the unknown

An animal in a hostile, competitive world needs to know at once whether a strange new shape can be ignored or must be dealt with by fight or flight. Until there is an explanation which is at least adequate enough to enable one to decide between these choices there is a strong feeling of insecurity. One might feel that it would be better to ignore something new unless one was forced to react. By then it might be too late. In practice it is extremely difficult to ignore something *before* it has been explained away. This need to explain is very strong if the new shape dominates attention and does not have to be sought out. And the need to have the right explanation is much more than the idle curiosity of exploration.

Once an explanation has been put forward there seems to be a very strong need to have this explanation confirmed as being right. At the end of every lecture which included the black cylinder experiment the first question *always* was: 'What made the black cylinder fall over?' This was not unexpected for the black cylinder may well have been the most interesting part of the lecture. But what was unexpected was the very fierce resentment that arose when I declined to explain the mechanism. At first I declined simply because I did not want the details passed on to a future audience. But the resentment was so fierce that I became interested in it for its own sake. Some people tried to trick me into revealing the explanation by asking cunningly worded questions but others became rude and offensive. On one occasion there was a suggestion that I should be physically prevented from leaving the room until I had revealed the explanation. Several attempts were made to spirit away the bag in which I kept the cylinder. Usually the lecture host was asked to worm the secret out of me and then pass it on.

In itself the mechanism could not have been of any more interest than an ordinary conjuring trick. Those who could not think of an explanation at all might have been slightly curious about how it was done. But those who had provided an explanation which satisfied themselves should have been content even if the actual mechanism was different. But it seemed that these were the people who most needed to know if they were right.

Education and being right

Throughout education the need to be right is drummed into one. The whole motivation is based on this need to be right. If you do something right then the teacher approves, praises you and puts a little tick against your work. These ticks for being right are the immediate rewards which act like the grains of wheat used by Skinner to get pigeons to perform tasks as complicated as playing a miniature piano. Immediately after each correct action the pigeon was rewarded with a grain of wheat. In real life being effective produces its own reward. If you are an effective property developer you make money. If you are an effective lawyer you win your cases. But in school the natural rewards of effectiveness are absent. Instead there is the artificial 'crystallized' reward of the little tick that means you are right. But being right is not the same as being effective, for being right simply means doing things as they should be done according to some pre-set idea.

Alongside the reward for being right there is the awful shame attached to being wrong. Instead of the glorious tick there is the shameful cross. The cross means that you do not have teacher's approval. The cross means that you have to try all over again which is a bore. The cross means that you are stupid. The cross means that others can feel superior to you. The well-educated terror of being wrong creates the fierce need to be right.

Being right is a feeling

In theory you are 'right' if your idea is an accurate reflection of reality. In practice being 'right' is something quite different.

If you think that water put into a pan over a flame will boil and it does boil then your thinking has been *right*. If you think your girl-friend will come back to you after a quarrel and she does come back then your thinking has been *right*. If you think that the stock-market will rise and it does rise then your thinking has been *right*. If you think that the noise at night is not a burglar but a mouse in the store cupboard then your thinking is right – if it is indeed a mouse. In practice thinking involves coming to some definite conclusion *before* it can actually be checked out. You want your thinking about the stock-market to be right before it actually rises otherwise you make no money. You want your thinking about the mouse to be right before you have to get out of bed to go and have a look. You want to be right about your girl-friend in time to do something before she runs off with someone else.

In practice being *right* in thinking has nothing to do with reality. Being right means *believing that you are right at the time of thinking*. This is completely different from checking your thinking against the actual reality when this becomes possible. Being right is the *feeling* of being right because this is what one acts upon. If you feel you are right and you really are right your feeling is no different than if you feel you are right but are actually quite wrong. You do not act upon the rightness of thinking in so far as the thinking fits reality. You act upon the *feeling of rightness* whether this corresponds to reality or not.

The previous chapter was concerned with basic mistakes in thinking. If one could avoid all mistakes in thinking should this be the best way of being right? In theory it might be. But not in practice. In practice one can feel *absolutely right* even when one is making the most awful mistake. No one ever makes a mistake deliberately. You make a mistake because you *feel* you are right. It is only afterwards that you find it to be a mistake – or someone else points out the mistake but you do not listen. Avoiding all mistakes in thinking does not make one feel any more right than if one had made mistakes. In practice the feeling of being right is a very real thing. It is much more concrete than the simple avoidance of mistakes or the matching of your ideas with reality.

Four ways of being right

Four basic ways of being right are discussed in this chapter. The human mind uses one or other of these ways to *know* that its thinking is 'right' enough for action or for imposing on other people.

100

R–1 Emotional rightness (currant cake)

If you read political journals you will come across articles which soundly argue a particular point of view. A journal of different political flavour will just as soundly argue the opposite point of view. In each case you can follow the soundness of the argument as it moves from point to point. Now and again data is brought in to support a point. The whole thing knits together. Then quite suddenly towards the end you find that the entire argument rests on some government being said to have a moral obligation to do something or other.

The purpose of a currant cake is to have currants in it. The rest of the cake is only there to keep the currants at a reasonable distance from each other. The cake acts as a sort of neutral matrix in which the currants are suspended. What really matters are the currants. The currants are the little goodies. There is no doubt about their value. They taste good and they are good. You know when you have come to a currant because the taste is unmistakable. And it would taste just as good to anyone else.

Goody-goody words are like the currants in a currant cake. There is no doubt about the goodness of such words. Their value is inbuilt and accepted by everyone. The words have long been established as convenient ways of saying: good, right, proper, ought to be done. The response to such words is emotional because they were set up in the first place as emotion capsules. Just as the cake is there to connect up the currants so you may have a long argument complete with logic and data simply as a device to allow you to proceed decently from one goody-goody word to another in order to build up a general emotional reaction.

Such goody-goody words include:

dignity
honesty

courage
justice
tradition
firmness
decisive
flexible
responsible

The value of the argument rests directly on the established values of such words. When you come to such a word you react to the emotional taste with which society has soaked the word. Just as the cake tastes nice because the currants taste nice so the argument feels right because enough goody-goody words have been properly worked in. It is quite easy to test this out by pretending to say 'boo'. You say 'boo' by refusing to acknowledge the taste of these goody-goody words and suddenly you find that the argument collapses. You can say 'boo' to historical tradition by calling it an obstacle. You can say 'boo' to courage by calling it foolhardiness. If you do this successfully then suddenly the thinking no longer seems right even though the logic and data are untouched.

In addition to these positive goody-goody words that taste so nice there are others that taste as bad as soda lumps in a cake. The process is, however, just the same. You put in the bad words and then your thinking about something seems right – you find you are hating what you are supposed to hate.

Words of this type include:

weak
degenerate
vacillating
cunning .
dishonest
opportunist
slick
aggressive

Gut feeling

It is perfectly legitimate to use words which act as emotional keys to unlock the feelings you need. Thinking is after all only moving from one idea to another in order to show how something which appears to be one thing can really be looked at in another way. So it is legitimate to work your way from one such word to another in order to make someone see the situation in a new way. Often, however, the feeling of emotional rightness does not depend on such words but is a direct 'gut feeling' that something is good or that something is bad.

It could be said that the only purpose of intellectual playing around is to get eventually to a point where you can react in a definite positive or negative manner. Any long political argument is meant to end with the 'gut feeling' which impels you to vote for the man and not to vote for his opponent. It is sometimes felt that since this gut feeling is there all the time the intellectual playing around is superfluous. What is usually overlooked, however, is that the gut feeling which seems so direct is actually triggered off by the choice of a particular word or line of thought. Gut feeling provides the power in the gun but the aim of the gun is intellectually controlled. A newspaper picture showing a frail pretty girl is likely to arouse the gut feeling that such a gentle creature should not be charged with murder. A slight change in camera angle, however, can show the girl as a 'brazen harpie or witch'. Intellectual playing around is rather like the camera angle because it puts things in the best way to elicit a particular gut reaction.

Gut feeling may seem a rather poor way of proving that our thinking about something is right. After all thinking is supposed to be there to free us from domination by raw gut feelings. And yet if man is going to use the products of his thinking there can be no better criterion of rightness – since his emotions are going to have to endure the result of the thinking. Emotional rightness is a perfectly valid way of showing a line of thinking to be right. In practice this is the

103

mechanism for being right that is used most often. There are, however, some severe limitations.

Limitations

1. The time-scale is likely to be the shortest possible one. If one uses emotional rightness it is difficult to look through something unpleasant in order to see something pleasant beyond it. Thus it may feel right to drop out of school and enjoy one's youth on the beach. If one used a longer time-scale one might see that future enjoyment depended on the interests and earning capacity that would have been developed at school. This short time-scale is a severe limitation since one of the main purposes of thinking is to free one from domination by immediate reactions in order to think ahead to what will happen later on.

2. Another limitation of emotional rightness is that the ideas it supports may clash with the interests of others. Since everyone has emotions everyone is entitled to his own emotional rightness in thinking. Thinking based on emotional rightness is only *right* for those whose emotions run that way. And it is absurd to try and impose this rightness on others.

Summary

Emotional rightness occurs when a line of thought triggers off that emotion which we are happy to have about something. It may be that the line of thought matches the emotions we already have on a subject. Or it may be that we simply enjoy the emotions that are aroused by the line of thought.

R–2 Logical rightness (jig-saw puzzle)

A man suspected of an armed hold-up is carefully questioned by detectives. They have no real clues to go on. But instead of clues they are hoping to find internal inconsistencies in the man's story. If he at first maintains that after leaving the football match he went straight to Joe's bar and remained there all evening but later is unable to confirm or deny whether there was a brawl in the bar then this internal inconsistency suggests that his story is wrong. On the other hand if his story fits together perfectly then it is deemed right even though it may actually be a complete invention. What matters is that the pieces should fit together without any contradiction – not that they correspond to reality.

In a jig-saw puzzle what matters is that each piece should fit in perfectly with the neighbouring pieces. The actual shape of each piece does not matter at all. If every piece fits perfectly then at the end you can be sure of having the completed picture. It is the same with logical rightness. There is logical rightness when each piece fits perfectly with the other pieces. If each fit is perfect then you can be sure that at the end the whole picture will also be perfect.

In a jig-saw puzzle you place the pieces one by one and all you have to ensure is that you are *right* at each step. This is what you have to do to be logically right in thinking. Be sure that you are right at every step. You must not make a single mistake or you upset the whole picture. The great advantage of this procedure is that it allows you to proceed step by step to conclusions which it would be quite impossible to check directly – but you know them to be correct because you have reached them by a correct path. You can reach such conclusions ahead of trial and error and even when trial and error is impossible. If each of your steps is right then your conclusions must also be right. It is like two spies arranging to meet in a strange place. One spy gets there first. Even if the spy fails to turn up he knows that he is in the right place because he has followed each instruction perfectly.

Funny-shaped pieces

In a jig-saw puzzle the pieces are not regular in shape but curved and indented to give funny shapes. This is not surprising because you make a jig-saw puzzle by pasting your picture on to a sheet of plywood and then cutting this up any way you want. No matter how funny the shapes are they must fit together since they came from the same piece in the first place.

In logical rightness the emphasis has shifted completely from the nature of the pieces to the goodness of the fit. The pieces are named-ideas (like freedom, table, government, codfish, etc.) but what matters is the logical way they are found to fit together. The whole Western intellectual tradition is based on logical rightness. Goodness of fit is all that matters. It is better to have some rather odd-shaped pieces which fit together perfectly than useful-shaped pieces which leave big gaps as they fit together. That is why classical philosophy has had so little relevance for everyday life. (Whether you have a 'transcendental ego' or not you do not get a discount when you buy fish.)

This exclusive emphasis on goodness of fit or logical rightness does mean that scholarship is too often the triumph of form over content. If one reads classical philosophy one is confronted with hugely elaborate systems beautifully worked out so that each piece fits smoothly with the next one. The validity of the whole thing rests entirely on this goodness of fit.

Choose your own pieces

Because logical rightness or goodness of fit automatically means that one is 'right' in one's thinking, one can construct the most bizarre systems which are nevertheless 'right' if the pieces can be shown to fit together neatly. A paranoiac has a fitted-together, logically consistent picture of the world which shows that everyone is indeed persecuting him. Various religious sects have logically consistent pictures of what life is all about. Astrology is a logically consistent picture of astrology. Alchemy is a logically consistent picture of alchemy.

In cutting out a jig-saw puzzle with a fret-saw you yourself choose how you are going to cut up the picture in the first place. Nevertheless when you have the puzzle and you put it together to give the complete picture you may still shout 'whoopee' when all the pieces fit. It is often the same with logically consistent systems. The picture of the world is cut up in a special way. This cutting up is the way we look at things, the named-ideas that we use. Then you fit these pieces together. Suddenly you find that all the pieces do fit. This means that your system is valid. So it is. But it is not uniquely valid. It is no more valid than any other way of chopping things up and then fitting them together again. The pieces you have in your system are only right within that system. You cannot take your own funny-shaped pieces as if they had an internal validity of their own and try and use them elsewhere any more than you can take pieces from your jig-saw and try and solve someone else's jig-saw with them.

Imagine an Eskimo igloo. Thinking of more southern houses you could say that it was made up of a domed roof which fitted on top of curved walls. You would be quite right for the roof and the walls would fit together to give the complete igloo. This would at once prove the validity of your choice of roof and walls as the basic ideas. But someone else would come along and say that this was nonsense because the igloo was obviously made of concentric rings placed one on top of another, each ring being smaller than the one on which it rested. He would make a model and show you how such rings did actually fit together to give an igloo shape. Yet another person would come along and laugh at all this elaboration. He would point out that the igloo was simply the visible half of a complete sphere the rest of which was buried in the snow ...

Make the pieces fit

In cutting out a jig-saw puzzle you may want a particular feature in the picture (for instance a face) to be on a piece by itself. Similarly in making up logical systems one may start out with a few pieces of fixed shape. These fixed pieces are the basic ideas around which one proceeds to put other pieces so that the whole lot will fit together to give logical rightness. Thus Freud constructed his system around the basic idea that sex was the prime mover in human behaviour. Since a sexual explanation of their behaviour often did not seem right to the people concerned it was necessary to construct the piece called 'resistance'. This 'resistance' idea indicated that some-one might refuse to accept the sexual explanation precisely because it was true. This meant that if an explanation was accepted it was true and if it was rejected it was also true. This is the mechanism by which logically consistent and impregnable myths arise. This does not mean that such myths are wrong. It simply means that the mechanism of logical rightness can easily construct systems which are impregnable whether they are right or wrong.

This process of making the pieces fit is of course the basis of the most *useful* type of human thinking. Certain ideas gradually establish themselves through common experience. These are the named-ideas that prove their usefulness (food, pain, control, love). In seeking to fit these ready-made pieces together one moves them around in various ways and even constructs special linking pieces until all the pieces can be fitted into a whole.

The danger is that the goodness of fit does nothing at all to validate the basic idea. What is more the choice of an initial basic idea can determine the whole system. For instance Western philosophy chose the importance of the 'self' as a basic idea and so developed a system that included reward/punishment, guilt/virtue, etc., to direct this self. Eastern philosophy on the other hand chose 'nature' as the basic idea

---

and then the self only became one particular knob on nature. Thus the self was no longer directed on a push/pull system but required to keep in harmony with nature.

In psychology we have the commonsense idea of memory which is where we store the information we have collected. By accepting this idea of memory psychology immediately commits itself to a particular type of system. Once there is a memory store then there must be some 'processor' to use that store. And the act of using we shall name 'recall'. This is a neat little system but it may totally prevent us from looking at the mind as a very different type of information system (for instance the one described in *The Mechanism of Mind*). There are many other commonsense ideas which are still holding up psychology. 'Motivation' is another one of them because it suggests something that happens before the action whereas it may actually happen after the action has happened in the mind.

Using the wrong pieces

Choosing a particular shape of a piece can determine the shape of other pieces as suggested above. But one can also get into trouble by fitting together pieces which do actually fit together but give the wrong answer.

Consider the following two problems:

A. A small bowl of oil and a small bowl of vinegar are placed side by side. You take a spoonful of the oil and stir it casually into the vinegar. You then take a spoonful of this mixture and put it back in the bowl of oil. Which of the two bowls is most contaminated?

The logical line of argument goes something like this: a spoonful of pure oil goes into the vinegar bowl but a spoonful of unknown mixture goes into the oil bowl (though the mixture is unknown it *must be* less than pure vinegar). So the vinegar bowl is more contaminated since it received more oil than the oil bowl received vinegar.

B. The chief needs some more warriors in his tribe to fight his wars. So he puts out an order that as soon as a woman has a female child she is to stop having any more children. Is he successful in increasing the ratio of boys to girls?

The logical line of argument goes something like this: there will be families with one boy, two boys, three boys, four boys, five boys, etc. But no family will ever have more than one girl. And there will not be any more one-girl families than some-boys families since a boy is just as likely as a girl to be born first. So there must be more boys than girls.

Both these solutions seem perfectly logical because the ideas fit together properly. But each of them is *totally wrong*. It is best to work out why they are wrong for oneself in order to appreciate the dangers of logical rightness.

Limitations

On the whole logical rightness is the most powerful and useful form of rightness. It has been responsible for man's achievements. Nevertheless there are some dangers:

1. Logical rightness is based not on the validity of the basic idea but on the way the ideas are fitted together. Incorrect basic ideas are made to seem right because they can be properly fitted into a logical structure. For instance the basic idea that illness is caused by too much blood leads logically to treatment by blood-letting which was used extensively in medicine until fairly recently.

2. No matter how impeccable the logical sequence may be the conclusions can never be more valid than the ideas one starts with.

3. A clever person can prove just about anything by skilfully fitting together in a logical manner whatever basic ideas he selects. Political arguments are usually logical structures which fit together selected and dubious basic ideas.

4. The very excellence of fit of a logical structure means that

a few incorrect basic ideas at the bottom of the structure can influence the shape of the whole. For instance the concept of guilt has strongly influenced Western psychiatry.

5. Logical rightness gives rise to arrogance and a belief in the absolute rightness of a particular line of thought. This absolute rightness means that the conclusions ought to be imposed on others who have not yet grasped this absolute rightness for themselves. Logical rightness is really confined to a chosen system with chosen basic ideas which are linked together in a valid way. The ideas and rightness are not transferable outside that system. Yet the arrogance that goes with logical rightness encourages one to transfer the conclusions to any other system.

6. Being right at each step is the essence of logical rightness. Yet this insistence on being right at each step is a very effective bar to creativity for creativity may involve being wrong at some point in order to move forward to a completely new idea (this is discussed more fully in the section on creativity).

In general the main limitations of logical rightness can be summed up as the arrogance which it produces and a failure to realize that logical fit is restricted to the particular basic ideas involved and does not even validate these.

R–3 Unique rightness (the village Venus)

If you have lived all your life in a remote village then the village Venus must be the most beautiful girl in the world because you cannot imagine anyone more beautiful.

The whole of science is based on this village Venus effect. Another name for the effect is 'unique rightness'. The village Venus has no rivals because the villagers cannot imagine anyone as beautiful – let alone more beautiful. She is unique. She has no rivals. Homage is all hers. Thus when a scientist cannot imagine an explanation which would fit the data as well as the one he has then he is convinced of the unique rightness of this explanation. The explanation has become a village Venus. This is not what the scientist tells himself. He tells himself that the rightness of his explanation arises solely from the way it fits all the facts. But actually the rightness arises directly from the uniqueness of the explanation.

If there were two rival explanations both of which fitted all the facts then a scientist would not feel happy with either of them. He would carry out further experiments to produce more data in the hope that this would favour one explanation rather than the other and so give him the unique rightness he needs. Two explanations both of which fit the data equally well are very useful but no scientist would feel happy that one of them was right. As suggested earlier Einstein's view of the universe offered an alternative explanation to the established Newtonian one. No scientist could be sure that either was right until an opportunity came to carry out an experiment which showed that Einstein's explanation was the unique one in explaining *all* the data. Today we have various alternative theories as to the start of the universe (big-bang, etc.) and astronomers are working hard to find data which will make one of these explanations uniquely right.

In science – as well as outside it – the inability to provide an alternative explanation *proves* the rightness of the available explanation. Any unique explanation is regarded as being right. If a red-haired man is seen at a bank robbery and a week later a red-haired man pays for a meal in a restaurant with one of the marked notes stolen from the bank then the unique explanation seems to be that he is indeed the bank-robber. It is only if your *imagination* generates the alternative explanation that perhaps the actual robber deliberately wore a red wig and deliberately paid over the marked notes to a red-haired man that the unique rightness of the first explanation suddenly diminishes.

de Bono's 2nd law

It may seem obvious that an explanation will be held to be uniquely right if there is no other explanation available. But it is a very fundamental process that has affected human thinking throughout history. The one possible explanation has always been regarded as the only possible explanation. What is really rather horrifying is that an idea which seems absolutely right in *itself* is actually only right because we have not enough imagination to think of an alternative. At first sight this is so obvious that it is easily overlooked and forgotten. That is why I feel it needs *emphasizing* with a special label.

de Bono's 2nd law:
'Proof is often no more than lack of imagination in providing an alternative explanation.'

The realization that proof does not arise solely from the excellence with which the explanation fits the facts but also from a feeble imagination is hugely important. It leads at once to three things:

1. It is not enough for scientists to be accurate and to work with painstaking logic on their data. They need to be imaginative and creative as well. It is creativity that turns up alternative explanations to challenge the certainty of a current explanation and so suggest new experiments.

2. No explanation can be absolute in its rightness since it is impossible to exclude an alternative explanation simply because you cannot think of one yourself and no one else can – at the moment.

3. People with feeble imaginations are the most sure of their conclusions.

If one puts the law in a rather fiercer form: 'Certainty arises only from a feeble imagination,' then one can clearly see the shift in emphasis from the solidity of a proof in itself to the

113

feeble imagination, which cannot provide an alternative explanation.

Soft sciences

In the hard sciences such as physics and chemistry one can set up an experiment to check a theory. In the soft sciences (sociology, anthropology, psychology, political science, economics, etc.) it is often difficult or impossible to do experiments. Instead of deliberate experiment one has to depend on careful observation. The trouble is that if observation is used to check a theory which has arisen from observation then this theory guides the new observation in a selective manner so you end up by seeing what you want to see. This danger is made worse because the soft sciences are fields in which one is in a furious hurry to come up with theories and explanations because these have immediate practical applications (sociology, economics, etc.). The result is that in these soft sciences de Bono's 2nd law operates to a frightening extent. The proof of definite theories is often no more than a lack of imagination in providing an alternative explanation for the observed facts.

In Mexico some huge, perfectly rounded stone balls were discovered on a hillside by an anthropologist. He had seen carved stone balls elsewhere and the artificial roundness of these new balls suggested at once that they had been produced by an ancient culture for some obscure ritual purpose. His imagination could not provide an alternative explanation. Fortunately he had a geologist friend who showed how the large balls were formed in cooling lava. Once this explanation had been thought of then it was seen that the available data (number of balls, disposition, several still embedded in lava) fitted it better than the anthropological one.

Of course the soft scientist (like anyone else) is perfectly correct in putting forward the explanation that seems right to him because it has unique rightness. Trouble starts when this explanation is then taken up by others who assume it is based on proof more rigorous than simple lack of imagination.

There is also the danger that having tied his ego to what was at first a tentative idea (until someone else provided a better explanation) the scientist vigorously rejects alternative explanations in order to preserve his position.

Outside science

Since unique rightness operates within science it is hardly surprising that it operates to an even greater extent outside. From among a number of possible explanations you can choose the best one quite easily. But you do not have alternative explanations unless you are given them or unless you generate them for yourself. If you cannot generate alternative explanations then you are forced to assume that your only explanation is uniquely right. This is what happened to Othello who was forced to believe the only explanation he could imagine and so to strangle Desdemona.

Unfortunately you can never be aware of what you are not aware of. What is worse is that if you cannot imagine an alternative then it is very difficult to *believe* in the possibility of an alternative explanation. Perhaps the best that one can do is to believe, unreasonably and even dogmatically, in the possibility of alternatives and a wider field of choice even if one cannot actually imagine any alternatives. At least this way one moves towards other explanations and is less rigid about the only explanation one has. The other thing one can do is to improve one's ability to generate alternatives by learning to think laterally.

Limitations

Emotional rightness (R–1) and logical rightness (R–2) both have real validity. Emotional rightness is when the line of thinking fits with one's feelings on the subject. Logical rightness is when the string of ideas do fit together properly. But unique rightness (R–3) does not have any real validity. What it does have is a great pragmatic usefulness. One does have to

115

use the explanations one has. One cannot sit about dithering in the knowledge that there are better explanations as yet unimagined. As with the other sorts of rightness there are limitations:

1. What is really only a tentative explanation for lack of a better one can quickly become dogmatic certainty. This certainty seems to be based on something much more solid than simple lack of imagination. This is particularly likely to happen when the idea is taken away from the originator and passed from mind to mind becoming less tentative with each passage.

2. Since a person can only feel sure that he is right if there is a unique explanation he may go to great lengths to demolish alternative explanations in order to strengthen his feeling of rightness. This is uniqueness achieved not by lack of imagination but by demolition of alternatives. This demolition attempt can take place even when the little evidence available fits all of the alternative explanations equally well.

3. The feeling that there can only be one true explanation leads to a refusal to accept alternative explanations which are simply different ways of looking at the same thing. This is like a person insisting that the only possible view of a house is the view from in front.

R–4 Recognition rightness (measles)

The child has a runny nose and a temperature. He feels ill and irritable. Eventually a blotchy rash appears. You send for the doctor who takes one look at the child and diagnoses measles.

The doctor diagnoses measles because he is sure that he can recognize the situation. The diagnosis is based on his feeling of 'recognition rightness'. He looks at the different symptoms and signs and finds that they add up to give the picture of measles. So he feels right in making the diagnosis. The name 'measles' simply means that the picture is so familiar and so well established that it has been given a name. So as soon as the doctor recognizes the situation he can slap on the name measles. Once he has got this name the doctor knows what is going to happen next (possible complications, cure of illness, etc.) and he also knows what treatment to use.

What diagnosis means is that a particular combination of features (special rash, temperature, runny nose, contact with other cases) unlocks a door called measles. A front-door key has a certain pattern of indentations cut into it. When this key meets a lock with matching indentations the door swings open. In effect the door 'recognizes' the key. It is the 'right' key. There is recognition rightness.

For this recognition rightness to come about there has to be a lock for the key to fit. This means that there must already be established in the doctor's mind a mental picture of measles. This mental picture would be built up through medical text-books, through seeing actual cases with a teacher who pointed out the significant features, and through experience. At first the young doctor would go through a sort of check-list before he could feel right about his recognition of measles: he would check off the blotchy rash, the runny nose, sore eyes, contact with measles, etc. If he was still not sure he might do some tests such as taking a blood sample which might either check on the measles or exclude other possible illnesses. All the time he is trying to match the mental picture of measles with the picture presented by the patient. As soon as he is happy about this he has 'recognition rightness'.

In botany class one spends hours trying to classify wild-flowers and other plants. You count the leaves and the petals and look at the shape of the stamen. At last you find that the combination of features unlocks a special Latin name which you proudly slap on the specimen feeling full of recognition rightness as you do so. With botany this recognition is the *aim* of your efforts. In real-life situations it is only the *beginning*,

117

for the purpose of diagnosing a situation is to enable you to know what to do next.

Recognition rightness is very important because it is really the basis of all action. As soon as you can recognize a situation you can take appropriate action just as a doctor does when he diagnoses an illness. If you cannot recognize a situation then you have to try and understand it. This means looking at it in different ways or breaking it down into simpler parts until at last you do come upon something you can recognize. Understanding is simply the search for recognition rightness.

Immediate recognition

The novice doctor recognizes measles by ticking off the features just as a botany student ticks off the features of the plant she is trying to name. But the experienced doctor takes one step into the room and at once proclaims 'measles' in a decisive and lofty manner which implies that any fool could have recognized what it was without having to bother him. You recognize a friend's face at once without having to tick off all the features. But if you wanted someone to meet your friend at a foreign airport then you would have to list the features: receding hair, squat nose, piercing blue eyes, etc.

Worked-up recognition

When recognition is not immediate one has to go to work on it. If you cannot at once recognize the mechanism that makes the black cylinder fall over you may want to pick it up, shake it, listen to it, try and unscrew it, etc., in an effort to find some more features on which to base your recognition. Medical tests and scientific experiments are attempts to generate more features in order to suggest an idea, to confirm an idea, to choose between ideas, or to exclude an idea.

At the end of your recognition efforts you come up with an idea which fits all the features you have found. This does not prove that your idea is right. What it means is that you have found a collection of features which are usually given a particular name and so you want to use that name and the action that goes with it. This cannot exclude someone else picking out different features and coming to a different conclusion just as one doctor may diagnose measles and someone else may come along and diagnose scarlet fever.

Enough

Recognition rightness means that you have so many matching features that you are sure your diagnosis is correct. You may want to act on the diagnosis yourself or (e.g. a politician) you may want to convince other people of the correctness of your diagnosis. If you do want to convince other people you list all the features which you find in the situation and which match up with the diagnosis you want to offer. For instance if you want to show that a regime is totalitarian you might list: lack of freedom of the press, no opposition party, imprisonment without trial, police permits for movement, etc. Some of the features might actually be part of the *definition* of the diagnosis (e.g. strawberries in strawberry flan) while others might be features which are usually accepted as indicating the condition. Thus the isolation of the measles virus would be part of the definition of measles but a slight rash and runny nose would only be circumstantial evidence.

If you actually list all the features that are part of the definition then you can obviously be sure that your recognition is absolutely correct. But in practice one matches up just enough features to feel that the recognition is right – this is recognition rightness. Because of this you may feel that you have recognition rightness but may be making a misfit mistake (M–3) as described in an earlier chapter.

Limitations

With recognition rightness there are several *degrees* of rightness. You may be sure of your diagnosis, very sure, certain, absolutely certain. You may feel certain on some occasions and only able to make a good guess on others. Recognition rightness is a very practical matter. You may have to act without being able to examine all the features you would like to examine because they cannot be obtained or because you have to act in a hurry (as in giving a quick blood transfusion on the battle-field). There are a number of limitations to recognition rightness:

1. The feeling of rightness or certainty is almost inversely related to the accuracy of the recognition. A person who feels sure about the recognition does not bother to collect further features and so tends to be wrong. On the other hand a person who is hesitant goes on collecting more and more features and so makes his match better and better.

2. Even if your recognition rightness is based on the examination of a good number of features you can never be sure that if you examined a few more you would not have to change your diagnosis completely.

3. You may genuinely only notice those features which give a particular diagnosis for a situation but someone else may be able to pick out from the same situation other features which give a different diagnosis. For instance what you call a Fascist regime someone else might call democratic. This danger is bad enough when you can examine the situation for yourself and have an open mind. It is even worse if you start with some diagnosis you would like to use. It is almost impossible to get an accurate diagnosis if you cannot examine the situation but have to rely on the features that have been picked out for you by someone else, e.g. a journalist.

4. The diagnosis names or patterns have to have been established beforehand otherwise there is nothing to recognize. If you have only a limited number of established

diagnoses then every situation will be recognized as one or other of these. In the old days the term 'leprosy' included a number of skin diseases for which we have since established separate identities. Similarly if you have only two categories, right-wing and left-wing, then you will recognize that people do fall into these two classes.

5. You have to be sure that the diagnosis name you use has the same meaning for other people. For instance the 'laurel' leaf is apparently much used for cooking on the Continent. But the 'laurel' leaf in England is highly poisonous. It is not that digestions are different but that a different leaf has the same label. Similarly what a person involved in the stock-market might call a slump (i.e. a levelling off of the fast rise in prices he would like to see) an ordinary investor might call a reasonable capital appreciation.

6. In order to be sure of your diagnosis you have to exclude other diagnoses which are fairly close. Thus in diagnosing measles the doctor would have to exclude German measles, scarlet fever, allergic rash, etc. But if you do not already *know* about these other possibilities (or cannot think of them at the moment) then you would be sure about a diagnosis which might in fact be incorrect. Thus it would be seriously wrong to treat scarlet fever, which needs a specific antibiotic, as measles, which does not. The danger here is close to that of unique rightness.

7. Even if your recognition rightness is perfectly correct this tells you no more than that the situation in front of you matches the named and familiar picture you have in your mind. Recognition rightness does not in any way prove that the basic picture is itself right. Thus if you have basic pictures of 'Imperialist', 'hippie', 'Communist', 'intellectual' you may be able to apply these diagnoses with ease but this does not validate your idea of what these labels mean. If you choose to call every bottle of tomato ketchup a dangerous weapon then you will indeed have recognition rightness whenever you call a bottle of tomato ketchup a dangerous

121

weapon. And you will be right when you go into a café and find it full of dangerous weapons. But you will not have proved that a bottle of tomato ketchup is a dangerous weapon.

Once an explanation has been put forward there seems to be a very strong need to have this explanation confirmed as being right.

Being right is the feeling of being right because this is what one acts upon.

In logical rightness the emphasis has shifted completely from the nature of the pieces to the goodness of the fit.

The mechanism of logical rightness can easily construct systems which are impregnable whether they are right or wrong.

In science – as well as outside it – the inability to provide an alternative explanation *proves* the rightness of the available explanation.

The awful thing is that you can never be aware of what you are not aware of.

Recognition rightness is very important because it is really the basis of all action.

8

The YES / NO System

Without doubt our most important thinking tool is the NO device. NO is an extremely effective tool. With this tool we can indicate that an arrangement of ideas put together in our mind cannot be allowed for one of three reasons:

1. The ideas do not fit together properly.
2. The arrangement of ideas does not reflect experience.
3. We simply do not like the ideas.

Having decided this the next step is to throw out the ideas. NO provides us with a powerful rejection tool. And as soon as one has a rejection tool one automatically has a *selection* tool since what is not rejected is'thereby accepted. A selection device is one of the two most fundamental requirements in any information handling system (the other fundamental requirement is a 'change' device).

As an abstract logical tool NO would not be much use but NO is brought into everyday use in a very practical way by being attached to physical feelings.

1. Fear is built up through training in the use of NO. If a child does something wrong he gets a smack and a NO together. At school being wrong results in a NO and the teacher's disapproval. NO becomes an emotional reaction rather than a neutral indicator.
2. NO is also based on a natural mis-match reaction which occurs when something is different from what we know it should be. This reaction is a very real thing, and some people

actually feel nauseated if they are shuffling through a pack of cards and come across an eight of hearts which is black instead of red.

As a thinking tool NO is so effective and so much part of our lives that we take it for granted and regard it as a natural part of thinking. Yet in its way NO is an artificial and even a rather peculiar information device for a biological system. It is possible to have systems of thought and language which have a different base. But NO is the device we have chosen and developed.

The four different ways of being right that were listed in the previous chapter are all situations which cannot be attacked with the NO device. Emotional rightness (R–1) means that an idea gives rise to a definite emotional reaction which supports the idea – it can never be denied that this is the case if it is so. You cannot tell someone that the sight of a hungry child does not really upset him if it does. Logical rightness (R–2) means that the ideas fit together or follow each other in a way that cannot be denied. If all shellfish give you a rash and a prawn is a shellfish then you cannot deny that a prawn will give you a rash. Unique rightness (R–3) means that the only explanation which fits the facts must be right. It is impossible to deny this unless you can produce an alternative explanation which is at least as good. You cannot deny that the sun goes round the earth until you come up with the alternative idea that perhaps the earth goes round the sun. Recognition rightness (R–4) means that you have recognized a situation. You are right in your recognition until someone comes along and shows how some feature does *not* match. In short if you can prevent someone from using NO to attack your thinking then you must be right.

Limitations

The YES/NO system has huge advantages (practicality, speed, decisiveness, sequence building, etc.) but it also has limitations which are sometimes overlooked.

1. *Adequate is good enough*

When you put forward a solution to a problem and receive the answer NO this means that your solution will not do. In practice it means 'Go on offering solutions until you come up with one which cannot be met with NO.' When you offer an answer to a question and receive the answer NO this also means that you must *go on* and find other answers. It is like taking a wrong turning on your way to some destination – the NO label at the end of the lane tells you to go back and try another road.

But as soon as you find a solution or an answer which cannot be met with NO then your effort is over and you stop trying. Once you have reached an adequate answer it becomes impossible to use NO as a propelling device to make you go on thinking. And yet beyond adequate or 'good enough' answers there can be answers which are very much better – *if only one looked for them*. But the NO device is useless for pushing one beyond the adequate answer.

2. *Permanent labels*

NO is used as a tool to block a line of thinking so that one can explore other pathways. NO is used at the time of thinking. But just as a criminal once convicted remains labelled as a criminal for the rest of his life so an idea rejected by NO may be permanently labelled as impossible. Even when circumstances change and the once rejected idea becomes feasible it is difficult to remove the NO label and look at the idea again.

Float glass as an idea was firmly rejected at the beginning of the century. This apparently was not known by the research scientist who re-thought the idea and made it work so very successfully that it is being adopted as the main process for making flat glass all over the world.

Ideas build on one another. The permanence of the NO label may mean that a current idea is actually based on an original rejection which was justified at the time but is no longer so. Thus many religious food taboos were soundly based on hygienic principles: for instance pork can be a particularly dangerous food to eat because it quickly deteriorates in a hot climate and it also harbours many parasites. But with refrigeration and carcass inspection in developed countries that basis for rejection is no longer valid.

3. *Sharp polarization*

The YES/NO system provides a very sharp watershed between what is rejected and what is accepted. Something is either right or it is wrong. It is perfectly possible to make up a smooth scale which moves from absolutely right at one end to absolutely wrong at the other: e.g. absolutely right, fits the facts better than anything else, probably right, possibly right, doubtful, does not feel right, seems wrong, wrong at first sight, wrong, definitely wrong, throw it out at once, absolutely wrong. One could choose other steps on the scale. Language could cope with this sort of scale. But in practice it is rarely used in thinking which prefers to have only the extreme ends of the scale: a definite YES or a definite NO. This comes about quite naturally. If something can be rejected then you do not want to waste time thinking about it any more so you throw it out. If something is acceptable you have to act upon it and if you are going to act upon it you might as well be confident that it is absolutely right since you cannot have half an action or half a decision.

A fisherman is sorting his catch into two baskets. Into the basket marked 'for sale in the market' he puts the best fish. Into the other basket 'for the local cats' he puts fish which are damaged or have gone bad. Some quite good fish end up with the very bad fish in the cat basket while some not so good fish end up with the very good fish in the market basket. If the fisherman had had a third basket marked 'doubtful', 'for the family' or 'worth looking at again' then this basket would have taken those fish which were neither good enough to be accepted fully nor bad enough to be rejected fully. In theory

126

we do have such in-between baskets (words like 'perhaps', 'possible', 'unlikely') but in practice we do not use them enough in thinking. We regard them as weak and ineffective and prefer to deal with definite ideas even if the matters we deal with are not definite.

This preference for sharp divisions means that we develop very 'hard-edged' concepts. Something either comes within the concept or else is right outside it. We do not say that a cat is a sort of dog or that a dog is a sort of cat. We say that a cat is a definite cat and definitely not a dog – and the other way round. If you want to treat cat and dog as similar then you must regard them both as 'animals'. But in practice the possibility of calling them both animals does not abolish the sharp division between cat and dog. The two ideas are still there. And one tends to use these ideas rather than the idea of 'animal' because one always goes for the most precise idea. Thus calling white men and black men both 'men' does not abolish the sharp distinction so well as a degree of overlap in colour as is the case in Brazil.

4. *Arrogance of righteousness*

The arrogance of righteousness which is probably the most dangerous fault of human thinking arises directly from the YES/NO system.

The arrogance of being right

'The cylinder *must* contain something which changes the centre of gravity over say a 20 min. period.'

'The object wouldn't fall over until the centre of gravity is outside the base. This was not seen to happen. Therefore the object *must* have been pushed from below.'

'The base of the black cylinder was of such an angle that it would be *bound* to fall after a lapse of time.'

127

'Draught from the door – *sure* it's a basic reason.'

'The *only* factor influencing its action (barring unseen, built-in mechanisms) was temperature. This *must* have caused something heavy within the cylinder to rise to the top thus disturbing the balance.'

'There are *only* two possibilities: either a change in weight distribution in the cylinder itself or a change in the cylinder base.'

During the experiment the audience was given no opportunity to examine the black cylinder so one might have expected the explanations to be very tentative. Yet in many of them one finds phrases like: 'must be' or 'only factor' or 'only possible explanation'. In conversation about the cylinder the declarations were even more dogmatic. It was as if the person was seeking for an absolutely solid base on which to start building and had to be sure of this solidity first.

The 'certainty' was usually of two types. The first was the unique rightness type. Here an explanation is offered as the only possible explanation simply because the viewer could not think of another one. In one of the examples given above the *only* factor outside the cylinder was temperature. Yet other people suggested sound, wind, vibration, bullets, etc. The last example declares there are 'only two possibilities' and yet leaves out the possibility that the cylinder might sag and fall.

The second type of certainty is based on logical rightness. In the second example given above the conclusion is that the cylinder must have been pushed from below. Yet there are many other possible solutions such as collapse of the base, loosening of an adhesive holding a basically unstable cylinder upright – even if one does accept the first two steps in the reasoning. And even these two steps may be wrong for under certain circumstances a heavy weight suddenly hurled against the side of the cylinder could knock it over. This is the suggestion reached in the logical sequence used below: 'A lateral force is required to knock the cylinder over. Since no lateral force was applied to the outside of the cylinder wall it must have been applied to the inside. Hence a weight on a compressed spring must have been suddenly released and hurled against the opposite wall of the cylinder or some similar mechanism.'

There is nothing wrong with this logical sequence, but the conclusion that the cylinder must have been knocked over by a 'lateral force' hitting against the cylinder wall on the inside leaves out a whole lot of other possibilities such as a collapse of part of the cylinder base, etc.

Ideas first

Logical sequence is fine as far as it goes. But it cannot go beyond fitting together in a sound way basic ideas that are already available. The danger is that the excellent way in which these basic ideas are fitted together gives rise to an arrogant sense of righteousness. What is worse is that once there is this sense of righteousness there is no further effort to explore other possible ideas. This means that unique rightness (R–3) is now added to logical rightness. It is interesting to note that in the black cylinder experiment only *one out of every ten* viewers suggested that there might be an alternative explanation to the one they put forward.

Intellectual tradition based on arrogant righteousness

The Western intellectual tradition has very largely been based on arrogant righteousness. The basic notion is that it *is* possible to be absolutely right and that one can achieve this sort of rightness through logical sequences. Throughout the ages philosophers have insisted on the absolute rightness of conclusions reached in this way. It is then felt that the absolute and inevitable rightness of such conclusions makes it *unnecessary* to look for other possibilities – and also provides a firm base for action. It is felt that once you have got to this

129

absolute rightness or 'truth' then further playing around with other ideas is superfluous since at best it could only get you to exactly the same place.

The major defect of this intellectual tradition is that although it appears to be based on logical rightness (R–2) it is really based on unique rightness (R–3). The development of a particular set of basic ideas and their manipulation into a coherent logical structure makes it appear that these are the only possible ideas. For instance basic ideas like 'ego', 'cause and effect' and 'time' seem to have an absolute validity and yet they only depend on unique rightness (because we have not developed other concepts to look at these things in a different way). Anyone who has done experiments in thinking cannot fail to be impressed by the fierce arrogance that arises from a correct logical sequence. It is impossible in these cases to point out that the rightness of the conclusion is confined to the particular ideas which have been used in the first place. It is only too easy to start with an assumption and then feel it is proved by the excellence with which it is handled.

Types of arrogance

In its extreme form the arrogance of absolute righteousness can manifest itself in many ways. Three of the most common forms are listed here:

1. *No alternatives:* There is only one possible way to look at things. This way is so right and so unique that one does not bother to look for other ways and can dismiss such other ways as being wrong even without examining them.

2. *No change:* A particular idea is so perfect that it is beyond change or improvement.

3. *No escape:* The idea is so absolutely right that everyone must work their way towards it. Lack of acceptance of the idea can only be due to ignorance, stupidity or bad will.

Arrogance, effectiveness and fanaticism

Single-minded belief in the absolute rightness of an idea is by far the most effective basis for action. This arrogance of belief gives four things:

1. A definite criterion by which to judge actions and so choose the best.
2. Relief from the necessity of considering other points of view let alone looking for them.
3. The right to impose a particular point of view on others.
4. Reasons for action above the conflicting demands of immediate self-interest.

The effectiveness of single-minded fanaticism can be seen in political leaders, religious leaders, military leaders, business leaders, etc. Today (as at any other time) the absolute arrogance of left-wing politics is matched by the arrogance of right-wing politics with each complaining about this characteristic in the other – and each being right. It is only fair to observe that just as man's worst behaviour to his fellow men has arisen from arrogance so his progress has often arisen from the same sort of arrogance. Advances in science have often been held back by an arrogant refusal to consider a new point of view and yet progress has often been brought about by an arrogant belief (even to the point of crankiness) in a new point of view when everyone else disapproved.

It hardly needs saying that arrogant righteousness and certainty have nothing at all to do with the validity of the ideas put forward. It is possible to be arrogantly certain about the most ridiculous of ideas. One of the major characteristics of lunacy is an impregnable certainty with regard to ideas that are crazy to everyone else.

Nor does arrogance have much to do with the number of people who hold the idea. There is almost an inverse relationship. If a large number of people hold an idea then the different expressions of it mellow the arrogance. But if only a

131

few people hold the idea then the cohesion of that group purifies the idea and this process is further helped by the outside opposition of others. Nothing is more damaging to the arrogance with which an idea is held than partial agreement. An idea which seemed preposterous when seen from the outside seems most reasonable when fitted into its logical context within the system.

Arrogance and stupidity

The most characteristic feature of stupidity is not inability to think or lack of knowledge but the certainty with which ideas are held. This certainty which easily reaches the level of arrogance is based on unique rightness (de Bono's 2nd law: Proof is often no more than lack of imagination). The sheer absence of alternative points of view makes the only point of view seem absolutely right. When this unique point of view happens to have emotional rightness as well then it is held with even more certainty.

I would go so far as to suggest that a person who was incapable of arrogance would be incapable of stupidity. Perhaps that is something education should be looking into.

Justified arrogance

Although the feeling of absolute rightness is characteristic of human thinking there is only one place where it is justified. This is when one is working within a *closed system*. There is a closed system when one starts out by setting up certain basic ideas. The conclusions that are then derived from these ideas are absolutely right within this artificial system.

Mathematics is an obvious example of a closed system. You set out by deciding to call two oranges 'two' and two groups of two oranges 'four'. You can then find that two plus two are four or that twice two are four. You can be absolutely sure of these things because you yourself have set up the system in the first place and all that follows is implicit in what you have set up.

Once one is within a closed system then one is justified in being arrogant about one's conclusions provided that no mistake has been made. It is like inventing a game of cards and following the rules one has set up for oneself in the first place. The danger arises when one treats as closed systems what are really open systems (for instance the way man looks at the world and forms his basic ideas about it). If one does make this mistake then one tries to behave with the arrogant certainty which is only applicable within a closed system.

Arrogant righteousness and the thinking process

The paradox is that man's need for absolutes, for certainty, and for fixed ideas in his thinking is exactly opposed to the way the mind works as a biological system. Biological systems work through change and evolution not through categorical choices followed by static states. In evolution an animal species that becomes too precise and fixed and static soon dies out because the process of change has come to an end. Ideas, like animals, are attempts to cope with the environment. The more absolute and fixed an idea the less chance it has of evolving. A biological system is always seeking to change and improve through experience of the environment. A static system on the other hand can only survive if it becomes a closed system and controls all aspects of the environment in which it operates.

The difference between a biological system and a static one can be seen in education. Education tends to be a static system because it prefers to follow fixed demands and fixed ways of satisfying them (curricula, exams, etc.). This works when education is regarded as a closed system which sets its own criteria of success and then satisfies them. But if one looks at education as a biological system which should be adapting

133

itself to the changing needs of society then the fixed ideas become a hindrance rather than a help.

The need for absolutes and certainty arises from a variety of factors among which are:

1. The need to have a fixed destination towards which one works.

2. The need for some unchanging standard to help decision-making and judgement.

3. The need for universal and unchanging ideas to make personal behaviour consistent with the behaviour of others.

4. The need for the security that arises from knowing one is right.

These are all practical points which affect behaviour. The problem is to combine the need for stability with the need for fluidity.

Complete fluidity means chaos. Yet complete rigidity means fossilization. The important point here is that in itself rigidity is an absolute whereas fluidity is not. Once you admit the possibility of fluidity and change you can choose a rate of change which allows enough stability for practical action and enough change for evolutionary progress. But if you choose rigidity then this precludes the possibility of change at all. You can slow down the speed at which you drive a car but a statue is never going to move.

The arrogance mistake

The need for certainty arises from the nature of the YES/NO system, from the desire to have a firm basis for action, and from the urge to bring a train of thought to a definite end. The aim is to provide a definite cut-off which fixes the idea or conclusion. Once fixed there is no question of exploring other alternatives or of developing the idea further. This fixing mechanism is the arrogance-clamp described in a previous chapter (chapter 6). Though this fixing of an idea does have a certain practical usefulness it can easily become the must-be mistake (M-4) described in the earlier chapter. This happens when what should be enough certainty in an idea to allow action becomes an absolute certainty in the idea for its own sake.

Doubt

The opposite of arrogance may seem to be doubt. It must seem that if one is not allowed to be certain of anything then one is reduced to impotence and dithering indecision. Clearly it must be better to act and risk being wrong than to do nothing at all because one can never be certain of being right. This is true enough but it is possible to distinguish two sorts of doubt.

1. *Retardant doubt:* This is 'slow-down' doubt. One is unsure of the rightness of action or even what action to choose. It is like refusing to take a bus because you are not sure where it is going.

2. *Propellant doubt:* This is 'speed-up' doubt. Here one moves forward very readily without the need for a fixed certainty about the rightness of the action. One does what seems right and is ready to change if change is required. It is like making the best guess possible as to where the bus is going and then jumping on in the knowledge that one can get off again if it proves to be the wrong bus.

Retardant doubt restricts action. Propellant doubt speeds it up because you do not need to wait for certainty. If you are prepared to change, adjust and improve your action as you go along you are much freer to act than if you have to be absolutely sure before you start.

Anti-arrogance

One is not really looking for the opposite to arrogant certainty. It is not a matter of finding opposites but of diminishing unjustified arrogance. If clothes are black with dirt you do not seek to bleach them white. What you seek to do is to restore them to their natural colour by removing the dirt. So one seeks to remove the arrogance which stifles thinking. One of the ways of doing this is humour, which is discussed in the next chapter.

Nothing is more damaging to the arrogance with which an idea is held than partial agreement.

I would go so far as to suggest that a person who was incapable of arrogance would be incapable of stupidity.

Without doubt our most important thinking tool is the NO device.

The arrogance of righteousness which is probably the most dangerous fault of human thinking arises directly from the YES/NO system.

It is only too easy to start with an assumption and then feel it is proved by the excellence with which it is handled.

9

Humour, Insight and P O

'The black cylinder fell over due to a bird or a clockwork mouse.'

'Tube fell over: 'cause concealed clockwork mouse with suction-pad feet climbed up tube – becomes top-heavy and falls over. Clockwork mechanism was silent.'

'Midget inside the black tube drank whisky and fell over so upsetting tube.'

'It died.'

'It got bored and fell asleep.'

'There was a little man inside and he wakes up every 20 minutes and stretches. One arm is longer than the other. This causes the cylinder to be pushed harder on one side – so it falls over.'

'Fell over – divine intervention.'

'A spider was swinging on a string from the top of the cylinder. Eventually he went too far, hit the side and knocked the thing over'.

'Exhaustion.'

'The black cylinder actually stayed where it was and the room tilted.'

'Indian rope trick, new version.'

'It is drunk.'

Could there really be a midget inside? Or even a mouse? Would a spider swinging on a string be heavy enough to knock it over? Could the cylinder really be exhausted, drunk or bored?

Are these explanations right?
Are they wrong?
Or are they just meant to be funny?

Escape from the YES/NO system

Humour provides an escape from the rigidity of the YES/NO
system. An explanation that is meant to be funny is no longer
judged as right/wrong within the YES/NO system because it is
outside that system. Humour has its own rules. In humour
you are allowed to say things which are obviously wrong or at
best unlikely. For instance you would be unlikely to find a
midget small enough to fit into the black cylinder. A midget
would be as unlikely as a full-sized person to have one arm
shorter than the other. Even if the arms were unequal in size
the push on the cylinder walls would not be unequal. Even if
the midget did push harder on one wall this would not topple
the cylinder over. Yet the explanation is funny because it does
have a surface plausibility. The explanation has meaning for
we can see the crazy logic involved. The ideas do fit together as
ideas even though they do not reflect reality.

There is a crazy logic when the cylinder is compared to a
man who would fall over if he was drunk or bored (with the
lecture) or just died.

Half right

The humorous explanations are half funny but half right as
well. The suggestion that a mouse would climb to the top for
cheese or that a tiny man would climb a ladder to the top are
only different ways of moving a weight to make the cylinder
top-heavy (even though this would not work, it was a mechanism chosen by a large number of viewers). If you started off
with the idea of a tiny man climbing a ladder then you could
later substitute the idea of a weight moving up a spiral driven
by an electric motor.

Push ahead

Because humour allows one to say things that would not otherwise be allowed one can push ahead with an idea under cover of humour and then catch up with it. From the idea of a spider swinging on a rope one could move on to the idea of a weight hitting against the side of the cylinder as suggested in many explanations. Alternatively one could move on to the idea of a swinging pendulum or rotating weight which would make the cylinder wobble more and more until it fell over. From the idea of the cylinder as a drunken man who fell over one could take the idea of the man's legs giving way and move directly from this to the idea of part of the cylinder base becoming flabby and collapsing.

Humorous ideas can act as *stepping-stones* towards an idea that makes a lot of sense.

Intermediate impossible

An 'intermediate impossible' is an idea which is not right in itself but which one uses as a stepping-stone to get to an idea which is right. The mouse climbing up for cheese, the swinging spider or the drunken cylinder could all be used as intermediate impossibles.

Right at each step

The very essence of the logical process of thinking is that you *must* be right at each step. By being right at each step you can be *sure* that your conclusion is also right even if you cannot check it in any other way. This is an immensely useful process because it allows you to move ahead in your thinking with the confidence that you are bound to reach a right answer if you go on being right at each step. From this logical process has arisen the tradition that *all* thinking must be logical and that one must be right at each step.

But if there are times *when you can tell at once* that the

conclusion is valid then there is no need to be right at each step because you no longer need to prove the validity of the conclusion in this way. If you lose your watch you know that you will recognize it as soon as you have found it without having to prove it is yours. Quite often in problem solving one is well able to recognize whether a solution would work from examination of the solution itself and not by the way it was reached. In invention or design you reach the idea first and then you set about finding whether or not it will work. There are a great number of thinking situations where the usefulness of the conclusion is quite independent of the way it has been reached. In these cases adherence to the rules of logical thinking does not especially help – and can be very inhibiting since logic is not creative. Instead of logical thinking one uses lateral thinking which allows one to proceed in a much freer way to find a solution which is justified after one has found it. In lateral thinking the use of intermediate impossibles is routine.

Insight

As soon as you can see the point of a joke the whole thing becomes obvious. You do not need anyone to 'prove it' to you or even explain it. You laugh at a joke because you are suddenly able to switch over and look at things in a different way.

Halfway through a lecture the professor saw a student look at his watch. The professor looked at his own watch – and then held it to his ear.

In this example it is quite easy to see how the professor indicated to the student that if he was impatient to be gone the professor was even more impatient.

You laugh at a joke because you are suddenly able to switch over and look at things in a different way. Insight involves exactly the same switch-over process as humour. You have been looking at things in a certain way and suddenly you are able to switch over and look at them in a new way. The new way *at once* makes sense just as the joke is *at once* funny when you have made the switch-over. In fact if an 'insight' solution is suddenly given for a problem which is not funny people do burst out laughing. This often happens with the problem given below:

Problem

In the singles division of a knock-out tennis tournament there are 111 entrants. The organizer wants to calculate the minimum number of matches that must be played. What is this number?

When this problem is set most people grab a pencil and paper and start working upwards from the 111 entrants and finding what happens at the end of the first round, second round, etc. A much simpler way which requires no pencil and paper and takes only a few seconds involves an insight switch-over. Instead of working towards the gradual selection of the winner consider instead all the eventual losers. There must be 110. Since each loser can lose only one match there must be 110 matches.

de Bono's 1st law

Insight is a hugely important process in human thinking. This is because the mind works by establishing fixed ways of looking at things. Such patterns become more and more established and get larger and larger. Insight is the only mechanism we have for escaping from established patterns and realizing that things can be looked at in a new way. As more information becomes available the old way of looking at things, the old idea, cannot make the best use of it. The idea has to be up-dated through an insight switch-over.

This need for insight switch-overs to up-date ideas arises directly from the behaviour of a patterning system such as the

141

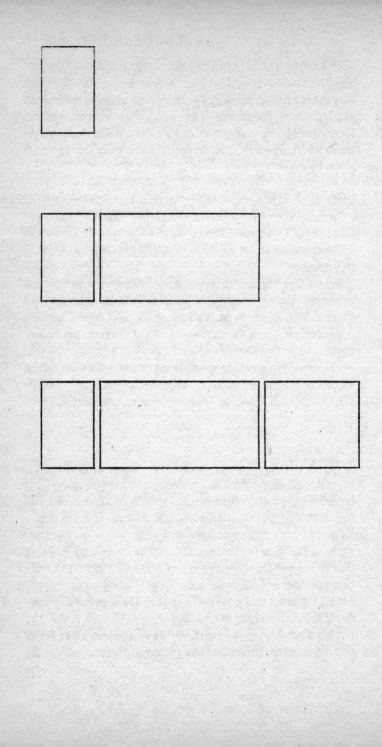

mind (see *The Mechanism of Mind*). This need is the basis of de Bono's 1st law:

'An idea can never make the best use of available information.'

Since an idea develops slowly over time as more information becomes available the idea cannot make as good use of that information as would be possible if all the information had become available at once. It is much easier to build a new block of flats than try to convert an old house.

If you give a person two plastic pieces as shown on the opposite page and ask him to make a shape that is easy to describe he will arrange them as shown. If you now add a third piece he will add this on. But if he has all three pieces to start with he makes the simple square shape (which is much easier to

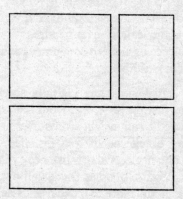

describe than a rectangle since the ratio of the sides does not have to be described).

Because the sequence in which information arrives will determine the way it is put together as an idea it is always possible to re-structure the idea and put the information together in a new way.

Discontinuity

An insight switch-over involves discontinuity. It involves breaking loose from an established way of looking at things in order to find a new one. For this reason insight cannot be achieved by the sequential process of logical thinking which insists that you must be right at each stage. 'Being right' means putting things together *as they should be put together* and that means according to the *established* way of looking at things. So logical thinking will only preserve this established way of looking at things – not change it. To do this one needs lateral thinking. But once an insight switch-over has come about then – *in hindsight* – logical thinking can show why the new way of looking at things is perfectly valid. Consider the following two points of view:

'Modern communications such as telephones, cars, aeroplanes bring people together as never before. Instead of communicating only over a few hundred yards one can now maintain communications over hundreds of miles.'

'The excellence of modern communications serves to keep people apart as never before.'

The first statement seems logically sound whereas the second seems just perverse. Yet from the second statement one can proceed to an insight switch-over in which one sees that the very excellence of long-distance communication means that one neglects short-distance 'village type' communication. Because one has friends all over the place one does not bother any more to make friends next door. And in the end short-distance communication is really more satisfactory since in a village you are always bumping into friends without having to make a special effort and they are there when you need them. All this is quite logical – once you have made the insight switch-over.

'PO' the new word

The thinking tool NO is the basis of logical thinking. By making it possible to reject what is wrong it allows one to be right at each step. Just as NO is a thinking tool the new word PO is a new thinking tool – but it has a completely different function. PO is a tool for discontinuity, insight, humour. PO allows one to step *outside* the harsh rigidity of the YES/NO system as one does with humour.

Placed before a statement PO indicates that the statement is being used as an intermediate impossible. This means that the statement may actually be wrong but is being used as a stepping-stone to new ideas. Without a device like PO (or humour) you would not be permitted to make the statement at all if it was wrong. PO is a crystallization of the escape function of humour.

'PO the black cylinder fell over because it is made of solid wood and an army of termites marched across the table and chewed away the base in so uneven a manner that the cylinder fell over. These were special invisible termites.'

From this intermediate impossible one could go directly to the idea of the cylinder falling over because part of its base had disappeared (e.g. through collapse, escape of air from an inflated pocket at the base, melting of a piece of ice which was supporting one side of the base, etc.).

Two uses of PO

These two uses are really but different aspects of the same basic function of PO: to counteract the rigidity, arrogance and sterility of the YES/NO system.

First use: liberation

A statement may have logical rightness (R–2) and it may also have unique rightness (R–3). The result is that the statement is regarded as being absolutely right. PO is used to challenge this absolute rightness and to show that it is but one way of looking at things. PO is used to liberate one from the rigidity of a fixed point of view. PO works outside the YES/NO system. PO does not imply 'that statement is wrong' or 'that statement is right'. PO (applied to a word, statement, argument, etc.) means: 'That is one point of view, that is your point of view starting as you do from certain basic ideas. I accept it as your point of view but I challenge it as the only possible point of view. Let's try and look at things in another way.' PO is really an invitation to escape from a particular point of view and to move laterally to generate alternative ways of looking at a situation.

'For the cylinder to fall over there *must* be a shift in the centre of gravity.'
'PO!'
'All the troubles in the world today are due to moral degeneracy.'
'PO!'

Second use: provocation

Even if an idea is wrong in itself it can serve as a starting point for a new line of thought or as a stepping-stone to get from one idea to a new one. PO can be used to set up such intermediate impossibles as:

'PO to reduce pollution a factory should be downstream of itself on the river.'

This seems ridiculous but by setting up this intermediate impossible one can move directly to the idea of having the factory inlet pipe from the river downstream of the outlet pipe so it is virtually downstream of itself and must therefore be much more careful of the muck it discharges. PO protects intermediate impossibles so that one can use them to reach a position which could not have been reached had one stuck to logical sequences. From this new position it may be possible to see things in a different way.

For instance there is the famous paradox about the man who comes up to you and says:

'I always tell lies.'

If he does always tell lies then he is telling the truth at the moment so he cannot always tell lies. One can use PO to say:

'PO he is not talking about himself but about his twin brother.'

If he is telling the truth his twin must always lie. But if he himself is lying on this occasion then his twin may likewise lie sometimes and tell the truth sometimes. So now he and his twin can come together again as a single person who sometimes lies and sometimes tells the truth.

If a statement can be rejected outright then PO may be used to protect it for a short while so that it can still serve to start up new ideas. In short PO allows one to do anything one likes with ideas in order to provoke new ones. In poetry one uses words and images to set off ideas and not as accurate analytical descriptions. PO is a provocative device to perform the same function in ordinary language.

'PO cars should have square wheels.' Then they would be so uncomfortable to ride that people would only use them when absolutely necessary.

Change and new ideas

PO is a creative tool which helps one to change to new ideas. This change may come about through escape from the old idea when this is no longer regarded as being absolutely right (liberation function of PO). The other way change can come about is through the generation of new ideas which provide alternatives to which one can move (provocation function of PO).

Humour provides an escape from the rigidity of the YES/NO system.

An 'intermediate impossible' is an idea which is not right in itself but which one uses as a stepping-stone to get to an idea which is right.

Insight is the only mechanism we have for escaping from established patterns and realizing that things can be looked at in a new way.

10
Imagination

Imagination is a big and useful word. Precise definition is difficult and the usefulness of the word is not increased by such definition. There seem to be four aspects of imagination:

1. Picture vividness

This means that if one is asked to imagine a person or a scene one is able to do so with great vividness. You can imagine Aunt Emma so precisely that you can see the way her nose twitches as she talks. You can imagine the fishing harbour from your holiday so vividly that you can see each individual boat tied up by the waterside café. Vividness implies *richness* of detail. Instead of just a blurred impression you can pick out all the features.

2. Number of alternatives

If you ask someone to give you all the ways he can think of for cooking an egg he might list: boiled, fried, scrambled. Someone else would add: baked, omelette. Someone else might add poached. A person who could give the whole list at once might be said to be more imaginative than someone who could name only three. It is not a matter of having knowledge but of getting to that knowledge. In practice it is very difficult to distinguish imagination from knowledge. If you ask someone to give you all the girls' names beginning with 'S' he might mention ten: Sue, Sally, Shirley, Samantha, Sara, etc. A girl at school might be able to remember far more by just thinking of her friends. So memory, knowledge and imagination are all mixed up here. But as in the first case the important thing is the *richness* with which one is able to respond to the question. In the first case it was the richness of detail, here it is the richness of alternatives.

3. Different ways of looking at something

This means coming up with different ways of looking at something. For instance someone might say that a bottle is half full of milk, someone else might say it is half empty, someone else might say the bottle is full of a mixture of milk and air.

4. Creative imagination

This involves fantasy and the ability to picture something which has not been experienced directly. It is a matter of putting things together to create a new experience. This aspect of imagination is discussed more fully under the creativity section.

Imagination in the black cylinder experiment

In the black cylinder experiment all types of imagination were involved in trying to explain what made the black cylinder fall over. Only one person out of ten offered more than a single explanation but the explanations offered by different people varied enormously. When you look at the variety of these explanations you realize how very limited is a single person's imagination.

The ideas offered become obvious once you have seen them but to think of these different ideas deliberately is very difficult.

An idea of the range of ideas offered can be given by taking a few definite features and seeing how different minds came up with different ideas:

Timing devices

One of the main features of the behaviour of the black cylinder was that it fell over *after a certain time*. It is fascinating to look at the different ways this delay was explained:

1. *No true time delay.* Something was done to the cylinder at the time it fell over (lecturer knocking it over or shaking table, an accomplice or someone shooting it down).

2. *Dependence on chance events.* The cylinder was only just stable so inevitably the draught from the door would at some time be strong enough to topple it over.

3. *Use of a predictable event.* This includes suggestions that the cylinder contained a mechanism which could be triggered off by laughter or that the breeze created when everyone lifted their pens at once would knock it over. Here the event is partially, but indirectly, under the control of the lecturer.

4. *Gradual Process.* Here a slow process was going on all the time until finally the effect was big enough to make the cylinder fall over. Such slow-moving processes included:

sand (falling slowly as in egg-timer)
lead shot (falling slowly, piece by piece)
wax melting
ice melting
fluid evaporating slowly
water flowing through fine capillary tube
treacle flowing
ball or rod moving through oil
friction device which slowed down movement very much
air escaping through a minute hole
ball travelling a long way down a spiral
weight being raised slowly on a fine rotating screw thread
expansion of slowly heated air
electrolysis producing gas slowly

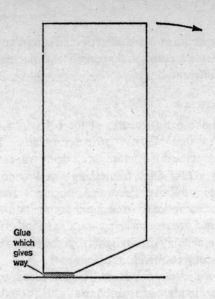

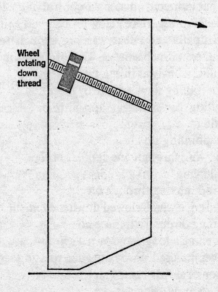

5. *Timing device.* In some ways this is similar to the previous group but here the slow process did not *itself* knock the cylinder over but simply *released* something like a spring.

clock
clockwork
electric 'timing device'

Raising weight to the top

Under the mistaken impression that it was enough to make a cylinder top-heavy for it to fall over, several explanations provided different ways of moving a weight to the top of the cylinder:

mouse with suction pads on feet climbing smooth wall
snail climbing up side
mouse climbing a ladder
weight floating upwards
insects collecting around a light at the top
weight moving up along a fine rotating screw thread
fluid evaporating and condensing in top
air pressure forcing fluid up
boiling fluid forced up as in a coffee machine
compressed spring slowly uncoiling and pushing weight up

Impact on side wall

Since the cylinder did not appear to be knocked over from the outside several explanations suggested that it was knocked over from the inside:

column falling against wall
rods leaning against wall one by one
spring (or elastic) hurling weight against wall
ball falling down a curved tube to hit against side
pendulum weight falling against side
magnet attracting a ball to one side through oil
midget drinking whisky and falling over

Alterations to base

A large number of explanations suggested that it was an alteration to the base that made the cylinder fall over. This alteration usually took one of two possible forms: something taken away from one side of the base or something added to the other side.

Taken away:
   ice which melts
   air which escapes slowly
   base snaps up on one side
   base made of material which collapses slowly under weight
   part of base made of wax which melts under heat of room (or by heating coil from battery).

Added to:
   pin pushed out by electric motor or electro-magnet
   temperature causes expansion of central pin so bulging base
   base made convex by opening up compressed spring
   balloon made to bulge out by increase in gas pressure (heat, electrolysis, or lead shot falling on another part of balloon)
   pin pushed down by weights falling in cylinder
   air pushed out

Reverse approach

Usually a particular approach seems so obvious that we cannot imagine the opposite approach achieving the same effect. There were several examples in the black cylinder explanations of people who took an approach which was exactly the opposite of the usual one.

Unstable to start with

The usual approach was to have a stable cylinder which was either knocked over in some way or which gradually (or suddenly) became unstable. Several viewers, however, took the opposite point of view and suggested that the cylinder was basically unstable to start with and that it was somehow supported and then this support gave way.

One type of explanation as suggested in the diagram on page 152 was for a cylinder with a cut-away base. This was held upright through being stuck to the table with wax (which eventually melted), with glue (which eventually gave way) or with a suction cap (which eventually came loose).

In another type of explanation the cylinder was also unstable but here the instability was compensated for by a weight put on the opposite side. This weight gradually moved across until the initial instability re-asserted itself and the cylinder fell over (as shown in diagram on page 152). The interesting thing is that this type of explanation would have made correct all those which simply indicated a shift of weight to one side as discussed on page 75.

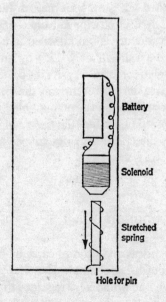

Battery

Solenoid

Stretched spring

Hole for pin

Bent to start with

Various explanations suggested that the cylinder gradually became bent in the middle and sagged over until the centre of gravity came to fall outside the base. One such mechanism used 'silly putty' which gradually deforms under pressure. Another used an elastic band to strain the cylinder and make it bend. Another used a pivot and shifting weight (see picture on page 33).

An opposite explanation suggested that the cylinder was basically curved but that the wall was made of wax-impregnated paper and so the cylinder could be warmed and straightened out before the experiment. In the heat of the lecture room the wax would soften and the cylinder would assume its natural form.

Turning a process off

Most explanations used electricity to make something happen: electric motors pushed up weights, magnets attracted weights or pushed out pins, heat melted wax. One explanation, however, used electricity in exactly the opposite way. The suggestion was that a pin attached to a spring was *held retracted* (see diagram on page 155) by an electro-magnet powered by a small torch battery. As the battery ran down the magnet would weaken until eventually the spring would break loose and push out the pin through a hole in the base of the cylinder, so upsetting it. Here the *failure* of the electricity is what produces the effect. This design also accounts for the time delay in a very neat way.

The use of imagination

The alternative ideas and ways of carrying out an idea listed above came from different minds. Had they all come from the same mind then one would have regarded that mind as highly imaginative. But what use is imagination? If you have imagination and can find five different ways of doing something and then pick out the best one, are you any better off than the person who has no imagination but arrived immediately at the best way?

Imagination and unique rightness

Without imagination one is apt to rely too much on unique rightness. If you cannot imagine any alternative explanations then it is easy to be convinced that the only one you have is absolutely right. As stated in de Bono's 2nd law: 'Proof is often no more than lack of imagination.'

Imagination and basic thinking processes

As suggested in an earlier section (page 55) the two basic thinking processes are: 'carry-on' and 'connect-up'. The fluency of both these processes depends very much on imagination. In the carry-on process the ease with which one idea follows on another depends on imagination. If you have the idea of using a pin to protrude from the base of the black cylinder then in your imagination you can quickly 'carry-on' the sequence of effect as the pin protrudes: pin protrudes . . . suddenly otherwise cylinder will incline over slowly . . . pin needs to be just long enough to tilt the cylinder so that its centre of gravity falls outside the base and it topples over . . . nor should the pin protrude too violently as this would make the cylinder jump up off the table and perhaps suggest the process . . . at the end with the cylinder lying on its side the protruded pin would be visible to the audience so it should either be needle-thin or else it should retract again. In order to carry on through these various considerations one needs to imagine clearly the behaviour of a protruding pin.

Similarly in the 'connect-up' process imagination gives a good spread to the starting point and the destination so that a connection is easy to find. For instance if the requirement is for some material that will slowly disappear an imaginative person will at once think of ice and dry ice. But he will also think that the material need not actually disappear but could shift (air or fluid escaping through a small hole from a flexible container) or change from rigid to flexible (wax).

Imagination increases the fluency of the basic thinking processes but does not by itself make them more correct or more useful.

Imagination and creativity

Imagination by itself is not creativity any more than numbers are mathematics. But it is one of the ingredients of creativity.

If you cannot imagine any alternative explanations then it is easy to be convinced that the only one you have is absolutely right.

Imagination increases the fluency of the basic thinking processes but does not by itself make them more correct or more useful.

Only one out of every ten viewers suggested more than one possible explanation for the fall of the black cylinder. Even this is a generous estimate, for anyone who even mentioned the possibility of an alternative (e.g. 'shift in centre of gravity or wind') was credited with two suggestions.

Some of the possible reasons for this low proportion of alternatives are discussed below.

1. *No time:* the time allowed the viewers was indeed short and with a longer time spent trying to think of alternatives there might well have been many more.

2. *Satisfied:* if you are satisfied with your explanation why should you bother to think of others?

3. *Thrown out:* a person may actually have thought of several alternative explanations but have thrown out those which he knew would not work. Someone else who was less discriminating would put down all the alternatives without realizing that most of them would be impossible.

4. *Too detailed:* a person who got involved in a detailed drawing of a possible mechanism would have little time to think of others. In any case the further one goes into detail the more difficult it becomes to move sideways to other explanations.

5. *Too general:* a person who was happy to stay at the first or second level of understanding (L–1, L–2) would not be able to offer alternatives since they would all come under the one general heading anyway. Thus 'it fell over' or 'there is a

device to make it fall over' would include all different ways of making it fall over.

6. *No knowledge:* to provide an explanation one would need some basic mechanical or technical knowledge. Complete lack of such knowledge would make it difficult to offer several explanations.

7. *No ideas:* finally it is possible that the failure to provide alternatives was due to a lack of ideas, to a lack of creativity in generating ideas.

All of the above reasons contribute to the process known as creativity. Creativity is usually the description of a result. If someone comes up with a sufficiently new idea or with a number of alternative ideas then he is said to be creative. But until the ideas come about there is a process of thinking which will bring about creativity. I prefer to call this actual process, as distinct from the result, *lateral thinking* which means moving sideways from one idea to another in a variety of ways which are not permitted by the rigid sequences of logical thinking. In this section the more familiar word 'creativity' is used to cover the process, the result and the attitudes of mind involved in generating ideas.

Purpose of creativity

The over-all purpose of creativity is to change ideas or produce additional new ones. These two processes are often mixed up together but they can be separated out as follows:

1. Escape from old ideas
2. Generation of new ideas

Satisfaction and creativity

If one has an idea which seems satisfactory why should one bother to try and change it? If you have a black cylinder explanation which works why bother to think of another one?

160

If you have an idea which you have been using satisfactorily in the past why try and change it?

The basic YES/NO system does not encourage one to go beyond the adequate, for as soon as an explanation is adequate then it seems to be as right as it can be. This rightness is further reinforced by the unique rightness process. This means that if an idea is seen to be right before any other ideas have appeared it gets treated as uniquely right.

Change

The three basic reasons for changing an idea in an apparently 'unnecessary manner' are the following:

1. Because you can see a fault in the current idea which others cannot see.
2. Because, without effort, your special experience or knowledge shows you an idea which is better than the current one.
3. Because you are simply dissatisfied with the current idea – but not because you can see a fault in it nor because you can see a better idea.

This unreasonable dissatisfaction is the basis of the creative attitude. It may be that you can look ahead to the possibility of a beautifully simple idea. Or it may be that you are dissatisfied by the clumsiness of the current idea. Either way there is an urge to find other ideas which goes beyond the satisfaction with the adequate which is all the YES/NO system requires. This attitude of 'good enough is not good enough' may arise for a variety of reasons: a sense of elegance or aesthetics, training or a deliberate habit of mind. Dissatisfaction may also arise for emotional reasons and even the ego-need to establish individuality by having ideas of one's own.

Knowledge and creativity

In the black cylinder experiment it is interesting that groups

161

which might have been considered creative in the artistic sense of the word actually provided fewer alternatives than other groups. In one art college audience the proportion of alternatives was 4 per cent and in another art college audience it was also 4 per cent. In an advertising audience it was 7 per cent. In a mixed technical and arts audience the proportion offering alternatives was 20 per cent. The average across all the groups was 10 per cent, so the art groups were below average and the technical group above average. This has nothing directly to do with creativity but with knowledge. If you are used to thinking in terms of magnets and screws and capillary tubes then you are more likely to provide a black cylinder explanation than if you are used to dealing with colour and texture and emotion.

Knowledge is *not* creativity but within any particular field it is difficult to come up with new ideas unless you have some ideas to play around with in the first place.

On the other hand too much experience within a field may restrict creativity because you know so well how things *should be done* that you are unable to escape to come up with *new* ideas. Furthermore too much knowledge means that you are unlikely to make mistakes by accident and unable to make them on purpose. In the black cylinder experiment very few of those who drew detailed designs offered alternative suggestions.

The relationship between creativity and ideas is suggested in the graph on page 163. This is *not* a graph of experimental results but simply a visual way of expressing what has been written above. Creativity rises steeply with increasing knowledge to a peak but then starts to fall off as a further increase in knowledge forces ideas into established channels.

Being wrong and creativity

The person who has five ideas but throws out four of them because they are wrong is going to appear much less creative than the person who has five ideas and keeps them all because he does not realize that they are wrong. In the section on imagination many of the alternatives suggested would never work. In simply counting the number of alternatives there is the danger of confusing the man who generates alternatives but throws them out with the man who never generates any at all.

Yet being wrong is often an essential part of creativity. This can happen in the following ways:

1. The new idea does not fit in with previous ideas and is therefore judged as 'wrong' (i.e. misfit mistake). In time it may be shown that the idea is actually right and that the framework of judgement has to be changed. But for that to happen you have to hang on to the 'wrong' idea for some time.

2. The wrong idea may continue to be wrong but may act as a stepping-stone to an idea which is perfectly valid. This is the intermediate impossible effect described earlier (page 139). One may realize that the intermediate impossible is wrong.

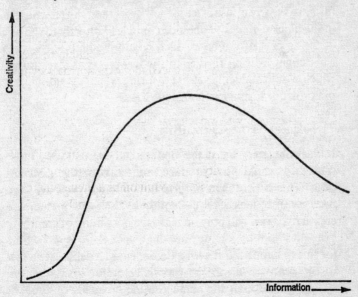

163

Or one may be unaware that it is actually wrong at the time. It is always possible to reject an idea as *soon* as it is seen to be wrong. But if you use PO to hang on to it just a little while longer then the idea can still be rejected in the end but has had more time to trigger off other ideas.

3. A mistake allows one to escape or get some 'distance' away from the established idea. This allows one to see the established idea more clearly since it is seen from outside. Even if one has to return to the old idea one retains this new perspective.

4. A mistake may ask a question that could not otherwise have been asked. (Pasteur's assistant made a mistake which so weakened a culture of cholera germs that it could no longer cause disease but instead led directly to an investigation of preventive inoculation against disease by means of altered germ cultures.)

In practice the most creative use of a mistake is as an inter-mediate impossible or stepping-stone to a new idea. For instance the wrong use of ice to melt slowly and shift the weight in the black cylinder to one side could lead directly to the use of ice as part of the base which would gradually give way. This might lead on further to the use of ice as a restrainer which would suddenly release a spring which would make a pin protrude through a hole in the base.

Techniques and time in creativity

It was suggested that if the viewers had been allowed more time they would have produced more alternative explana-tions. This is because a natural flow of creativity may have been *cut off* by lack of time. But time by itself will not increase creativity. Time will only increase the possibility of creativity brought about by a happy accident since there is more time for this to happen. But a long time spent in a deliberate effort to be creative will not be especially useful since one will simply go through the same routine channels of thought over and again. There are certain techniques and methods (of lateral thinking) which will increase the chances of creativity – partly through removing inhibiting habits of thought and partly through special settings which encourage the flow and rearrangement of ideas. Even so it is not the amount of time spent on such methods that matters but the ability to use them at all.

This unreasonable dissatisfaction is the basis of the creative attitude.

Too much experience within a field may restrict creativity because you know so well how things *should be done* that you are unable to escape to come up with new ideas.

12

Attention and Clues

One does not pay attention to everything. And one acts only upon what one is paying attention to. The reaction may be thinking or it may be action (which is only thinking that passes through our mouths or our muscles instead of our minds).

The world around is full of a huge number of things to which one could pay attention. But it would be impossible to react to everything at once. So one reacts only to a selected part of it. The choice of attention area determines the action or thinking that follows. The choice of this area of attention is one of the most fundamental aspects of thinking.

Area of attention

Even in the black cylinder experiment which appeared to be a single area of attention different people selected different parts for attention. Some people paid attention to events outside the cylinder itself and suggested it was shot at or knocked down by the wind. Others paid attention to the base of the cylinder and supposed that this altered. Others paid attention to the weight distribution of the cylinder.

Carving out areas of attention

Since one never reacts to the total situation at any one moment there is a process of 'carving out' the area that is to be attended to. This carving out process may take place in three ways:

in space (paying attention to only part of a scene)

in time (paying attention to only part of a sequence of events)

in depth (paying attention to only some details)

Different attention areas

It is obvious that a man who is talking about how to cook sausages is not talking about how to cook tripe. When attention areas are clearly different then there is no confusion. Confusion can also be reduced when two people actually decide that they are talking about different things even though there is some area of overlap. For instance a parent may be talking about the sort of education he wants for his *child* whereas the headmaster he is talking to may be considering the general education system that is best for *most* children. It is possible to agree that the child in question is not 'most children'.

The difficulty arises when the attention area appears to be the same but is actually different. This difficulty may arise for three reasons which are related to the three ways in which attention areas are set up.

1. There may be a difference in 'space', that is, the size of the attention area. Two attention areas may cover almost the same ground and still have parts which belong to one area but not to the other. For instance in considering hospital care the high cost of staff may come into the hospital's attention area but not into that of the patient though all other aspects of patient care may be included in both attention areas.

2. There may be a difference in 'time'. This may occur when one person is looking further ahead than another. For instance a person may feel that he has found a house at bargain price in a certain area. But his wife may point out that in

167

two years' time a huge block of flats is going to be built right in front and will cut off both view and light as well as making the neighbourhood more noisy.

3. There may be a difference in detail 'depth'. A man may want to buy a horse at an auction because it looks very handsome and he can imagine himself cutting a fine figure on the hunting field. But the horse expert at his side has looked more closely at the action of the horse as it moves and suspects it might be slightly lame.

In each of these cases the people are looking at situations which appear the same but are really different. The areas are different because they include different features. It is usually impossible to decide whether the different features are there because a different area of attention has been chosen in the first place or whether these particular features have been noticed and have created this different area of attention. This does not matter. What matters is that the different features create a different situation. When one is trying to understand an unknown situation these noticed features can be called clues.

Clues

A person who looks at the black cylinder as it lies on its side and knows that it has fallen over is not looking at exactly the same scene as someone who noticed that it fell over with a loud crash. The first person might go on to suggest that the cylinder was light enough to have been blown over by a draught from the door but the second person is unlikely to suggest this since he is looking at a 'heavy' cylinder. A person who observed that the cylinder fell over abruptly is not looking at the same scene as someone who missed the actual moment of fall. The first person would be looking at a cylinder containing a mechanism capable of producing a sudden change whereas the second person might include mechanisms that would allow the cylinder to sag or wobble before it fell over.

Generating clues

As in a detective story there are various sorts of clues. A few of the more common sorts are listed here:

1. Clues that are obvious to everyone – but may still be misinterpreted.

2. Features that are obvious to everyone but do not become clues unless some significance is attached to them.

3. Clues that are not at all obvious and have to be worked on.

The viewers were not allowed to examine the black cylinder. They were not allowed to pick it up, shake it, test its solidity, examine its base or anything of the sort. In fact some of them were so far away that they could not even see it clearly. It may seem that it was impossible to work up any clues at all. Several viewers, however, did notice points so minor that they were missed by most people and yet which could provide useful clues. Some of these points are given here:

'The lecturer seemed surprised when the cylinder fell over.' This at once suggests that he could not have made the cylinder fall over at a moment of his choice (e.g. by pulling it over with a fine nylon thread).

'The cylinder fell over quite suddenly.' This excludes a gradual tilting over, a crescendo wobble or a sagging change in shape. Many of the explanations suggested (e.g. 'silly putty' in the base) would have been excluded by this observation.

'The cylinder fell over with a bang.' This suggests the cylinder was quite heavy and difficult to knock over.

'The cylinder fell in a particular direction.' This might well have been significant, especially if related to the audience or lecturer.

'The lecturer appeared to be quite careful about how he placed the cylinder.' This suggests a falling mechanism which acts better in one direction than another or possibly the intention that the cylinder should fall towards the audience and so not expose its altered base.

'The cylinder was black.' Obviously noticed by everybody but of significance if it was felt that the black was used to absorb heat better.

'The cylinder was kept on its side before use.' In fact this was untrue but might have suggested a mechanism, e.g. a slowly moving semi-fluid substance which would coat one side and so compensate for a basic instability. On being stood upright the substance would move to the bottom so allowing the basic instability to knock the cylinder over.

'The cylinder was kept upside down before use and then turned over.' This might suggest a mechanism involving movement of fluid from one tank to another or an egg-timer effect.

'No wax or water was visible on the table after the cylinder had fallen over.' This excludes the idea of a basically unstable cylinder resting on an ice block or being stuck to the table with wax which eventually melted.

Purpose of clues

1. To suggest ideas

If you are trying to understand an unfamiliar situation then you look for clues which might give you some ideas. If you are a plane-spotter you might look at the shape of the tail. If you are an art collector you might look at the way the paint has been applied to a painting. As suggested in the section on recognition rightness (R–4), page 116, the doctor's first idea of a diagnosis is set off by the most obvious clues like the rash in measles. To generate ideas in this way it may be enough just to notice the scene but usually one has to concentrate on some feature and try and see its significance.

2. *To confirm ideas*

As soon as one has an idea or guess then one looks for other clues to see if the idea fits. When a doctor forms an idea of a diagnosis then he looks for other signs and symptoms and carries out some tests. For instance if he thinks the patient has a duodenal ulcer he may ask whether the 'indigestion pain' wakes the patient at night or whether it is relieved by eating food. Usually this search for confirming clues can take place in the situation itself. Sometimes it can only be done on the memory of the situation which has passed. For instance one might say: 'Did the black cylinder really wobble before it fell over?' This hindsight search is obviously not as satisfactory as an actual one.

3. *To exclude ideas*

As we have seen on page 85 the misfit mistake (M–3) arises when an idea just does not fit the circumstances. One can look for clues in order to prove that a current idea (one's own or someone else's) is wrong or at least needs modifying. Or one can look for clues in order to exclude several other possible explanations which seem to do just as well as each other. In this case one tries to make the choice by finding clues which show that all but one of the ideas can be excluded. Thus in the black cylinder experiment one could exclude the possibility that the lecturer knocked over the cylinder deliberately by the clue that the fall took him by surprise. One could exclude the possibility that shapes flying overhead were ducks because they were flying too high.

Shuttle

In practice one shuttles backwards and forwards between clues and ideas. The clues suggest ideas, reject them, confirm them, modify them. Ideas on the other hand tell one where to find clues, how to get them, what significance to attach to them.

Danger

The danger is that once you have an idea then it is easy to notice only those clues which fit in with the idea. There are situations in which a number of explanations are possible. If you settle on one explanation then it is easy to find enough clues to confirm that explanation. But someone else could find enough clues to confirm a quite different explanation. This is quite apart from the possibility of ignoring clues that do not support your ideas.

Science tries to be wrong

In theory a scientist's only aim is to prove himself wrong. He sets up an idea only in order to be able to carry out experiments which will show the idea to be wrong. This means he can move on to a better idea. And so the process is repeated. Of course if a scientist is quite unable to prove himself wrong then he is delighted but he still goes on trying because each time he fails adds to the value of his original idea.

In order to try and prove himself wrong the scientist spends all his time generating clues. That is the purpose of experiments which are situations designed to offer far more clues than could be provided by ordinary natural situations. The scientist goes as far into detail as he can. He is also very unwilling to come up with conclusions unless he feels he has gone as far as he can go.

Practical man has to be right

Unlike the scientist the practical man has to be right *as soon as possible* because he has things to do. The practical man is happy if he can get the car started in the morning as soon as possible even if it means pouring a kettle of hot water over the inlet manifold. The practical man goes into detail just far enough to give him an explanation to get on with. As soon as he has an adequate explanation that is good enough. It is hard to quarrel with this attitude because one does not have all the time in the world for doubt, indecision and further exploration (though this lack of time is too often used as an excuse for a disinclination to go beyond the adequate). The only thing one can quarrel with is the arrogance with which this 'practical' explanation is sometimes held. That a practical explanation may be more useful under certain circumstances does not mean that it is necessarily better than a deeper explanation.

Bandwidth analysis

When a man sits down to shake a couple of dice you cannot tell what numbers he is going to throw. If you could you would make a fortune at the Las Vegas crap tables. So one feels that it is a chance situation and one can tell nothing about it. This is how many scientists feel about situations where they do not have all the details. They feel that any attempt at explanation may be as much mystical guesswork as proposing to predict the throw of the dice by using the number of the automobile that nearly ran you down that morning.

Yet there is quite a lot one can tell about the man sitting down to throw some dice. You can be sure that the number he throws is not going to be more than 12 or less than 2. You can be sure that the number will fall within this 'bandwidth'.

If all you know is that a moving vehicle has wheels rather than legs you do not know much about it. But you can at once say that it can probably freewheel down slopes, that it would not be very good at climbing ladders or stairs or going over very rough ground, and that it probably cannot jump. Similarly with the mind, we do not know all the details of the nerve networks and chemical transactions but we do know enough about the type of information system involved to tell within a broad bandwidth the sort of mistakes the mind can make and the general way it handles information in thinking.

Bandwidth analysis is not a tentative guess such as a practical man may make when in a hurry. Bandwidth analysis involves taking whatever clues are available and finding the maximum use that can be made of them in constructing a broad but sharp-edged bandwidth of possibilities.

Distortion

If one has collected a lot of clues, does one try hard to find an unusual explanation to fit them all together? Or does one jump to an easy explanation and distort or ignore those clues that do not fit?

In practical situations one makes for the easy idea since ideas that fit are considered far more important than odd clues which do not. That is what gives human thinking the important 'blurry' quality that was discussed as being so useful on page 61. One's first impulse is to look at different things as similar rather than similar things as different. Thus an explanation which is almost right is regarded as right instead of being thrown out because some minor detail does not fit. A classic example of how easy it is to ignore something if it does not fit in with existing ideas is given by the discovery of the Barr bodies in cells. It was always assumed that cells from male or female animals were indistinguishable by appearance. The particles which were sometimes seen alongside the nucleus in some cells were dismissed as damage caused by handling of the cell. Scientists had been peering down microscopes at cells for a very long time before one of them realized that these particles were a characteristic feature of cells from females.

In the black cylinder experiment the loud crash caused by the cylinder as it fell over was ignored by those who suggested that a very light cylinder had been blown over by a draught of air.

13

Think–2

Starting place

The choice of attention area is of the utmost importance since it provides the starting place for thinking. You would be extremely surprised if two people starting from quite different places but following identical instructions ended up at the same place. Thus in thinking one often fails to realize that although the starting place *seems the same* it may be very different. One attributes the disagreement to faults in the thinking process which is often perfectly valid. The real cause of disagreement is the different starting place.

Disagreement

Disagreements may be based on different data available to the arguers or they may be based on any of the thinking mistakes such as magnitude (M–2), monorail (M–1), arrogance (M–4), etc. But by far the majority of disagreements are simply based on different starting places. It is like two witnesses in court describing the behaviour of the black car at the scene of the accident. They disagree entirely and call each other all sorts of names. In the end they find they are talking about two different black cars.

No matter how excellent the thinking itself may be, if the starting place is different the conclusion will be different. Indeed the better the thinking the more likely one is to reach a different conclusion. This is of course the basis for the miss-out mistake described earlier on page 90. Here different people start by looking at different parts of the situation but both feel that they are looking at the total situation and the same situation.

Think–2 is suggested as a different sort of thinking. Instead of assuming that one is talking about the same thing (just because one says so at the beginning) and then moving steadily from idea to idea trying to convince the other person of the validity of the argument, one turns away from argument by linked ideas. Instead each person carefully maps out the landscape of their own starting place. Thinking then becomes a matter of discovering where there is overlap and where there is distance. An attempt may be made to set up new areas which will include areas that are otherwise separate. In Think–2 one tries to find out where people *are* instead of trying to convince them of where they should be. For instance in a labour dispute the two starting landscapes might be as follows:

Union man:
his standing in the union
need to show some achievement
possibility of keeping the men with him
keep open future possibilities
push the management to greater efficiencies
this year's high profits and dividends
what is happening to workers in other fields
high cost of living
keeping up with inflation
present basic wage
overtime rates and overtime opportunities
a rival labour leader who has more powers of persuasion

Management man:
profit margins
his own status

his reputation as a hard bargainer
share prices, earnings per share, takeover bids, value of his own shares
next year's profits
market trends
last year's profits
possibility of absorbing costs somewhere
effect of increased price on market share
future strikes
support for current labour leadership or desire for change
newspaper publicity
pressure from Government to hold wages

Even such small differences as the fact that the union man is looking at this year's profits and the management man at last year's and next year's could have a considerable effect. All the factors listed above are normally taken into account by being worked into the argument (consciously or unconsciously) at some point. But in Think–2 one lays them out at the beginning so there is no struggle to work them in and no danger of them being hidden factors that though never mentioned dominate the argument. One may have to invent euphemisms for those areas which could not readily be admitted. For instance the existence of a rival labour leader might be disguised as 'stability in union structure' and management's personal status might be disguised as 'job effectiveness'. As long as both sides knew what the euphemisms meant it would not matter.

A father discovers that his daughter has been smoking pot and sits down to have a talk with her about it. They have different starting places and different 'pictures'. As used here a 'picture' is an image, a group of ideas that go together, a bundle-idea, a particular area on the starting map. The different starting maps might be something as follows:

Daughter:
only smokes it occasionally

177

does not ever seek it out
does not particularly like it
all her friends do it
does not want to appear square and old-fashioned
exciting and daring because it is forbidden
other smokers of pot seem quite normal
better than alcohol (no hang-over or sickness)
a passing phase
part of the youth world which is different from the adult world
father could not possibly understand the now-scene

Father:
taking drugs means taking drugs all the time
pot leads at once to other dangerous drugs like heroin and methedrine
once you start using chemical aids for your soul you lose control
keeping bad company, casual morals, promiscuity, disease
daughter will become drop-out and never settle down and marry
daughter easily influenced by others
disgrace if daughter goes to prison
failure as a parent
beginning of downward trend from which there is no escape
what sort of people could she ever meet in the hippie scene

It is obvious that the starting places are so totally different that the two are really talking about different things. The differences could be summarized as follows:

pot-smoking is abnormal and indicates drop-out/pot-smoking is normal and requires more effort to refuse than to go along with it
dangerous and bad for health/harmless and quite pleasant
what will happen next / live for the moment
rebellion against society/conforming to society

index of degeneration/a temporary fad in itself

From looking at this map of the starting places it is clear that the father is neither right nor wrong – and the daughter likewise. Each has a different starting map, a different point of view, different pictures. The severe limitation of ordinary thinking is that one proceeds only by deciding that one picture is wrong and another right. Having decided this one proceeds to the next picture. This again is judged as right or wrong. But this time the judgement is also based on how well the new picture fits in with the already chosen picture. In Think–2, in contrast, one accepts that the pictures *do exist* as they exist. One cannot make them cease to exist by judging them as wrong. In ordinary thinking one tries to reach a conclusion by making strenuous efforts to deny the right to exist of any picture that is judged to be 'wrong'. This judgement of wrong means that the picture as it stands does not fit in with the framework of the person judging – but of course indicates nothing about how it fits in with the framework of the person who holds the picture.

In Think–2 one accepts the existence of a picture as unalterable and instead of denying this existence seeks to extend the picture and construct bridges so that a person is no longer trapped within a particular picture but can move on to another idea. By judging a particular picture to be 'wrong' one not only fails to make it disappear but effectively isolates it and prevents one moving on to something else. In Think–2 one may well regard a particular picture as wrong but instead of rejecting it one accepts its existence and uses it as an intermediate impossible to move on to something better.

The basic principles of Think–2 might be set out as follows:

1. Map out the different pictures instead of assuming that they are the same.

2. Accept the existence of the different pictures and realize you cannot make a picture disappear simply by putting a NO label on it.

3. Try and develop new bridging ideas whereby one can move from one picture to a different one.

For instance in the example given above a bridging idea might take the following form:

'Instead of being cramped and constricted by society's demands one may want to be free and individual and sensitive and creative. Does a chemical prop achieve this? And if it does achieve this may it not prevent one developing these free qualities for oneself just as travelling in a car makes the leg muscles flabby?'

In Think–2 one finds the map and explores it. In ordinary thinking one tends to build the map as one feels it ought to be and decides the rest should not be there at all.

The choice of attention area determines the action of thinking that follows.

Most disagreements arise from the assumption that if the over-all picture seems the same for everyone then they are reacting to the same thing and it is only their thinking that is wrong.

In practice one shuttles backwards and forwards between clues and ideas.

The danger is that once you have an idea it is easy to notice only those clues which fit in with the idea.

In theory a scientist's only aim is to prove himself wrong.

Unlike the scientist the practical man has to be right as soon as possible because he has things to do.

In Think–2 one tries to find out where people are instead of trying to convince them of where they should be.

Conclusion

Even though he is going to see them every day a teacher finds it easier to recognize his pupils if he learns their names. 'John Smith' is easier to deal with by that name than as the 'boy with freckles who always brings frogs into the classroom'. Everyday thinking is also something we meet every day. Giving names to different aspects of it makes it easier to recognize these aspects as old friends or enemies. For instance one can recognize that one is making a magnitude mistake (M–2) or that someone you are talking to is using logical rightness (R–2) or that an article you are reading is working at the 'give it a name' level of understanding (L–3). The names are not meant to be jargon words which one flings around and uses to confuse things rather than make them more simple. They are just meant as handles with which one can hold on to certain ideas. The notation list (e.g. M–2, R–2, L–3) is suggested because eventually one may be able to use it instead of the name. In dealing with an article for instance it is much easier to jot down (R–1) in the margin opposite an emotional point than to write the name out in full.

In addition to dealing with such practical aspects of everyday thinking as being right, being wrong and understanding, the book has also explored thinking devices like black boxes, porridge words, the YES/NO system, PO, etc. A lot has been left out. A lot has been made simpler than perhaps it ought to have been. The purpose of the book has been to provide a practical way of dealing with everyday thinking. Everyday

181

thinking is very different from such idealized systems as mathematical logic and it is no use wishing everyday thinking was as precise. It is not and it probably never will be. One has to accept things as they are. Nor must one forget that some of the devices of everyday thinking (black box, porridge words) are in fact extremely useful devices even though they seem horribly vague and meaningless to the pure abstract logician.

Some of the things written in this book are very obvious. I have never felt that there is any danger in underlining what is obvious because very often the sheer obviousness of something means that it is paid no attention. For instance I think the village Venus effect is something that is obvious but cannot be emphasized often enough. Other things are not so obvious. This is always the danger when one tries to write simply. On the other hand there will be many things which a reader will notice and which I myself did not notice.

I hope nothing in the book has been set out as a dogma which must be agreed to or accepted. I only intended to suggest that there are ways of looking at things which can be useful. Anyone who does not find them useful need not use them. A garden shed is full of tools. You use whichever you want and leave the rest. But it is a good idea to look around and see what tools are there before you decide not to use them.

If I had to summarize the most important rules of everyday thinking I would reduce them to two.

1. Everyone is always right
2. No one is ever right

These are not contradictory. In his own mind no one is wrong on purpose. According to his knowledge, experience, emotions and the way he looks at things a person sets up his ideas in the best possible way. One has to realize that this is the case when one is dealing with other minds. It may be obvious but it is very easy to forget. If one does want to show someone a different point of view one has to arrange things so that his mind can of itself snap over to that point of view in an insight change. Insight is also the process by which one moves, oneself, from an idea that is adequate to one that is even better.

Although everyone is always right within his own context this rightness is not absolute but limited to that context. This means that one must forego the arrogance and dogmatism of those who feel that they are so right that they must impose their ideas on others. This arrogance is the most deadly mistake since it goes right against the natural behaviour of the mind in improving its ideas. If one accepts that no one is ever right in an absolute sense then one is more willing to look around for better ideas, and to look at the ideas of others.

Summary Notes

185

M–4 Must-be mistake (fixation of an idea by
    arrogant certainty).
M–5 Miss-out mistake (a conclusion from part of
    the situation is applied to the whole).

Two Basic Thinking Processes
1. 'Carry-on' (follow directly along a train of
   thought).
2. 'Connect-up' (set up a new point as a problem or
   a question and try to connect-up with it).

The Yes/No System
Faults:
1. No good for going beyond the adequate.
2. Labels become too permanent.
3. Hard-edged concepts and sharp polarizations.
4. Arrogance of righteousness.

Types of Arrogance
1. No alternatives.
2. No change.
3. No escape.

Doubt
Types:
1. Retardant doubt.
2. Propellant doubt.

The Creative System
Humour
Insight
PO
Imagination
Creativity

Clues
Uses:
1. To suggest ideas.
2. To confirm ideas.
3. To exclude ideas.

page 141   **De Bono's 1st Law**
'An idea can never make the best use of available information.'
   (Because information trickles into the mind over a period of time the idea patterns set up cannot be as good as if all the information arrived at once.)

page 113   **De Bono's 2nd Law**
'Proof is often no more than lack of imagination – in providing an alternative explanation.'
   (If you cannot think of a better explanation you are sure the one you have is right.)

page 145   **PO**
A new functional word designed to introduce the discontinuity function into thinking to help creative and insight changes. PO is as basic to lateral thinking as NO is to logical thinking.
Two functions of PO:
1. Liberation (escape from old ideas).
2. Provocation (generation of new ideas).

page 139   **Intermediate Impossible**
An idea which is wrong in itself but nevertheless serves as a useful stepping-stone to an idea which is perfectly valid.

page 88   **Arrogance-Clamp**
Used to fix an idea so that it can neither be developed further nor exchanged for a better idea.

page 61   **Sharp Brain**
Capable of immediate and fine discrimination (as in animals).

Blurry Brain
Coarse discrimination at first followed by fine discrimination later (as in man).

187

PRACTICAL THINKING

           Vague and apparently meaningless words which play
           a very important part in thinking.

page 67   Uses of Porridge Words:
           1. To set up questions.
           2. To provide usable explanations.
           3. Cross-links for thinking.
           4. To act as black boxes.
           5. To prevent too early commitment to a specific
              idea.

page 46   **Named-ideas**
           Any idea which can be referred to by a single name.

           Bundle-ideas
           Any group of ideas which are temporarily used
           together as a whole but which do not have a single
           name.

page 173   **Bandwidth Analysis**
           Establishing the broad statements that one can
           make with certainty about a situation even though
           one may not have the fine detail.

page 41   **Press-button Idiom**
           Producing the effect one wants by finding the right
           button to press and without having any knowledge
           of what happens in between.

page 40   **Black Box**
           Being able to use an idea or a machine effectively
           without knowing the details of what goes on inside
           (e.g. you can use a TV set without knowing anything
           about electronics).

page 45   **Leap-frog**
           Jumping over details you do not need to know by
           pushing them all into a black box or a porridge
           word.

188

page 49 **Requiron**
A single name given, for the sake of convenience, to
'that which is required' or 'that which we are
looking for'.

page 175 **Think–2**
Instead of proceeding from one idea to another as in
ordinary thinking (Think–1) you map out your
position. For instance in an argument instead of
using a train of linked ideas to convince the other
person of your point of view you both start by
mapping out respective starting positions and then
proceed by considering areas of overlap and areas at a
distance from each other. Think–2 avoids the
common difficulty that two people think they are
talking about the same thing when they are not.

The basic principles of Think–2 can be set out as
follows:
1. Map out the different pictures instead of assuming
   that they are the same.
2. Accept the existence of the different pictures and
   realize you cannot make a picture disappear
   simply by putting a NO label on it.
3. Try to develop new bridging ideas whereby one
   can move from one picture to a different one.

page 182 **Basic Rules of Everyday Thinking**
I. Everyone is always right.
(A person's ideas are always right in the context of
what he sees and the way he sees things.)
II. No one is ever right.
(In an absolute sense, for rightness is related to a
particular context, a particular set of ideas.)